THE BEAUTY QUEEN
OF LEENANE

Martin McDonagh

The Royal Court Writers Series published by
Methuen Drama in association with
the Royal Court Theatre

Royal Court Writers Series

5 7 9 10 8

The Beauty Queen of Leenane was first published in Great Britain
in the Royal Court Writers Series in 1996
by Methuen Drama

Random House UK Limited
20 Vauxhall Bridge Road, London SW1V 2SA

Random House Australia (Pty) Limited
20 Alfred Street, Milsons Point, Sydney
New South Wales 2061, Australia

Random House New Zealand Limited
18 Poland Road, Glenfield, Auckland 10, New Zealand

Random House South Africa (Pty) Limited
Endulini, 5a Jubilee Road, Parktown 2193, South Africa

Random House UK Limited Reg. No. 954009

Reissued with a new cover 1996
Reprinted 1997

The Beauty Queen of Leenane copyright © 1996 by
Martin McDonagh
The author has asserted his moral rights

ISBN 0 413 70730 X

A CIP catalogue record for this book is available from the British
Library

Papers used by Random House UK Limited
are natural, recyclable products made from wood grown in
sustainable forests. The manufacturing processes conform to
the environmental regulations of the country of origin

Typeset by Wilmaset Ltd, Birkenhead, Wirral
Printed and bound in Great Britain by
Cox & Wyman Ltd, Reading, Berkshire

The Royal Court Theatre &
Druid Theatre Company present

The Beauty Queen
of Leenane

by Martin McDonagh

A Royal Court and Druid Theatre Company co-production.

*First performance at the
Town Hall Theatre, Galway. 1 February 1996.*

*First performance at the
Royal Court Theatre Upstairs, Sloane Square. 29 February 1996.*

*First performance as part of **The Leenane Trilogy** at the
Town Hall Theatre, Galway. 16 June 1997.*

*First performance as part of **The Leenane Trilogy** at the
Royal Court Theatre Downstairs, St Martin's Lane. 18 July 1997.*

*The Royal Court Theatre is financially assisted by the Royal
Borough of Kensington and Chelsea. Recipient of a grant from
the Theatre Restoration Fund & from the Foundation for Sport
& the Arts. The Royal Court's Play Development Programme
is funded by the Audrey Skirball-Kenis Theatre. Supported by
the National Lottery through the Arts Council of England.
Royal Court Registered Charity number 231242.*

How the Royal Court is brought to you

The Royal Court (English Stage Company Ltd) is supported financially by a wide range of public bodies and private companies, as well as its own trading activities. The company receives its principal funding from the **Arts Council of England**, which has supported the Royal Court since 1956. The **Royal Borough of Kensington & Chelsea** gives an annual grant to the Royal Court Young People's Theatre. The **London Boroughs Grants Committee** contributes to the cost of productions in the Theatre Upstairs.

Other parts of the company's activities are made possible by business sponsorships. Several of these sponsors have made a long-term commitment. 1996 saw the sixth Barclays New Stages Festival of Independent Theatre, supported throughout by **Barclays Bank**. **British Gas North Thames** supported three years of the Royal Court's Education Programme. Sponsorship by **WH Smith** helped to make the launch of the Friends of the Royal Court scheme so successful.

1993 saw the start of our association with the **Audrey Skirball-Kenis Theatre** of Los Angeles, which is funding a Playwrights Programme at the Royal Court. Exchange visits for writers between Britain and the USA complement the greatly increased programme of readings and workshops which have fortified the company's capability to develop new plays.

In 1988 the **Olivier Building Appeal** was launched, to raise funds to begin the task of restoring, repairing and improving the Royal Court Theatre, Sloane Square. This was made possible by a large number of generous supporters and significant contributions from the **Theatres Restoration Fund**, the **Rayne Foundation**, the **Foundation for Sport and the Arts** and the **Arts Council's Incentive Funding Scheme**.

The Company earns the rest of the money it needs to operate from the Box Office, from other trading and from transfers to the West End of plays such as **Death and the Maiden**, **Six Degrees of Separation**, **Oleanna** and **My Night With Reg**. But without public subsidy it would close immediately and its unique place in British theatre would be lost.

Every Friendship is give and take

You give us £20 each year and a one-off initial joining fee of £25 and we give you:

*Two top price tickets for every production in the Theatre Downstairs for only £5 each

*Two top price tickets for every production in the Theatre Upstairs for only £5 each

*Priority booking for all productions at the Royal Court

*Free tickets to selected Royal Court readings and other special events

*You will also receive a newsletter including articles from writers, directors and other artists working at the Royal Court, and special offers for other theatres and arts events

AFTER JOINING YOU WILL ONLY HAVE TO PURCHASE TWO TICKETS IN THE THEATRE DOWNSTAIRS AND YOU WILL HAVE ALREADY SAVED £9

TO JOIN SIMPLY COMPLETE THE FORM AVAILABLE AT THE BOX OFFICE COUNTER

The Royal Court has a track record of success; I am associated with it because it is uniquely placed to take advantage of the current climate of optimism, energy and innovation.

Our plans for the transformed theatre in Sloane Square include the latest stage technology, a cafe bar and improved audience facilities enabling us to anticipate the latest in contemporary drama whilst at the same time the refurbished building will bear testimony to our past successes.

I invite you to become part of these exciting plans.

Gerry Robinson
Chairman, Granada Group

If you would like more information please contact me at the Royal Court Theatre, St Martin's Lane, London WC2N 4BG.

The Royal Court Theatre, Sloane Square, was built in 1888 and is the longest-established theatre in England with the dedicated aim of producing new plays. We were thrilled to be awarded £16.2 million in

Stage Hands Appeal

Royal Court Theatre

September 1995 - from the National Lottery through the Arts Council of England - towards the renovation and restoration of our 100-year old home. This award has provided us with a once-in-a-lifetime opportunity to bring our beautiful and important theatre up to date and redevelopment work is now in progress at our Sloane Square site.

However we have no wish for change for change's sake, and the key to our success will be continuity. The Royal Court's auditorium, for instance, has been an important factor in the success of the English Stage Company over 40 years. Nothing must be done to jeopardise that supportive relationship. Similarly, the recently improved facade is a much-loved and familiar face on Sloane Square. This will scarcely change. But everything else must and will, not simply because the structure is crumbling and the mechanical and electrical services outdated. The Royal Court building must evolve and change to both maintain its present well-earned position in British theatre and also to lead the way into the next century.

Building work in Sloane Square is now well underway, but one major problem remains: the Court must raise more than £5 million itself in order to complete the work. The rules of our Lottery award are clear: the Lottery will pay up to three quarters of the costs of the capital project but we must find over £5 million ourselves as Partnership Funding. To help reach our target, we have launched our *Stage Hands Appeal* which aims to raise over £500,000 towards this £5 million target from friends, audience members and the general public by the end of 1998. So far the appeal has met with great success, but the fact remains that we still have some way to go to reach our goal.

If you would like to help, please complete the donation form enclosed in this playtext (additional donation forms available from the Box Office) and return it to: Development Office, Royal Court Theatre Downstairs, St. Martin's Lane, London WC2N 4BG. For more information on our redevelopment project please call 0171 930 4253. For details on forthcoming productions in our temporary homes (at the Duke of York's and Ambassador's Theatres) contact the Box Office on 0171 565 5000.

TRUSTS AND FOUNDATIONS
The Baring Foundation
The Campden Charities
John Cass's Foundation
The Chase Charity
The Esmeé Fairbairn
 Charitable Trust
The Robert Gavron
 Charitable Trust
Paul Hamlyn Foundation
The Jerwood Foundation
The John Lyons' Charity
The Mercers' Charitable
 Foundation
The Prince's Trust
Peggy Ramsay Foundation
The Rayne Foundation
The Lord Sainsbury
 Foundation for Sport
 & the Arts
The Wates Foundation

SPONSORS
AT&T
Barclays Bank
Hugo Boss
Brunswick PR Ltd
Citibank
The Evening Standard
The Granada Group Plc
John Lewis Partnership
Marks & Spencer Plc
The New Yorker
Prudential Corporation Plc
W H Smith

CORPORATE PATRONS
Advanpress
Associated Newspapers Ltd
Bunzl Plc
Citigate Communications
Criterion Productions Plc
Dibb Lupton Alsop

Homevale Ltd
Laporte Plc
Lazard Brothers & Co. Ltd
Lex Service Plc
The Mirror Group Plc
New Penny Productions Ltd
Noel Gay Artists/Hamilton
Asper Management
A T Poeton & Son Ltd
The Simkins Partnership
Simons Muirhead and
 Burton

PATRONS
Sir Christopher Bland
Greg Dyke
Spencer & Calla Fleischer
Barbara Minto
Greville Poke
Richard Pulford
Sir George Russell
Richard Wilson

ASSOCIATE
Patricia Marmont

BENEFACTORS
Mr & Mrs Gerry Acher
David H. Adams
Bill Andrewes
Elaine Attias
Angela Bernstein
Jeremy Bond
Katie Bradford
Julia Brodie
Julian Brookstone
Guy Chapman
Yuen-Wei Chew
Carole & Neville Conrad
Conway van Gelder
Coppard Fletcher & Co.
Lisa Crawford Irwin
Curtis Brown Ltd
Louise & Brian Cuzner
Allan Davis
Robyn Durie
Gill Fitzhugh
Kim Fletcher & Sarah Sands
Winston Fletcher
Nicholas A Fraser
Norman Gerard
Henny Gestetner OBE
Jules Goddard
Carolyn Goldbart
Rocky Gottlieb
Stephen Gottlieb

Frank & Judy Grace
Jan Harris
Angela Heylin
Andre Hoffman
Chris Hopson
Trevor Ingman
Institute of Practitioners
 in Advertising
International Creative
 Management
Peter Jones
Thomas & Nancy Kemeny
Sahra Lese
Judy Lever
Lady Lever
Sally Margulies
Pat Morton
Michael Orr
Sir Eric Parker
Lynne Pemberton
Carol Rayman
Angharad Rees
B J & Rosemary Reynolds
John Sandoe (Books) Ltd
Scott Tallon Walker
Nicholas Selmes
Lord Sheppard
David & Patricia Smalley
Dr Gordon Taylor
A P Thompson
Tomkins Plc
Elizabeth Tyson
Eric Walters
A P Watt Ltd
Sue Weaver, The Sloane
Club
Nick Wilkinson

AMERICAN FRIENDS
Patrons
Miriam Blenstock
Tina Brown
Caroline Graham
Edwin & Lola Jaffe
Ann & Mick Jones
Maurie Perl
Rhonda Sherman

Members
Monica Gerard-Sharp
Linda S. Lese
Yasmine Lever
Leila Maw Strauss
Enid W. Morse
Mr & Mrs Frederick Rose
Paul & Daisy Soros

You have one week to live.

Out Wednesday
http://www.timeout.co.uk

The English Stage Company at the Royal Court Theatre

The English Stage Company was formed to bring serious writing back to the stage. The first Artistic Director, George Devine, wanted to create a vital and popular theatre. He encouraged new writing that explored subjects drawn from contemporary life as well as pursuing European plays and forgotten classics. When John Osborne's **Look Back in Anger** was first produced in 1956, it forced British Theatre into the modern age. In addition to plays by "angry young men", the international repertoire ranged from Brecht to Ionesco, Jean-Paul Sartre, Marguerite Duras, Wedekind and Beckett.

The ambition was to discover new work which was challenging, innovative and also of the highest quality, underpinned by the desire to discover a contemporary style of presentation. Early Court writers included Arnold Wesker, John Arden, David Storey, Ann Jellicoe, N F Simpson and Edward Bond. They were followed by David Hare and Howard Brenton, Caryl Churchill, Timberlake Wertenbaker, Robert Holman and Jim Cartwright. Many of their plays are now regarded as modern classics.

Many established playwrights had their early plays produced in the Theatre Upstairs including Anne Devlin, Andrea Dunbar, Sarah Daniels, Jim Cartwright, Clare McIntyre, Winsome Pinnock, Martin Crimp and Phyllis Nagy. Since 1994 there has been a major season of plays by writers new to the Royal Court, many of them first plays, produced in association with the *Royal National Theatre Studio* with sponsorship from *The Jerwood Foundation*. The writers included Joe Penhall, Nick Grosso, Judy Upton, Sarah Kane, Michael Wynne, Judith Johnson, James Stock, Simon Block and Mark Ravenhill. In 1996-97 The Jerwood Foundation sponsored the Jerwood New Playwrights season, a series of six plays by Jez Butterworth and Martin McDonagh and Ayub Khan-Din (in the Theatre Downstairs), Mark Ravenhill, Tamantha Hammerschlag and Jess Walters (in the Theatre Upstairs).

Theatre Upstairs productions have regularly transferred to the Theatre Downstairs, as with Ariel Dorfman's **Death and the Maiden**, Sebastian Barry's **The Steward of Christendom**, a co-production with *Out of Joint*, and Martin McDonagh's **The Beauty Queen Of Leenane,** a co-production with Druid Theatre Company. Some Theatre Upstairs productions have transferred to the West End, such as Kevin Elyot's **My Night With Reg** at the Criterion and Mark Ravenhill's **Shopping and F££€ing** (a co-production with *Out of Joint*) at the Gielgud.

1992-1997 have been record-breaking years at the box-office with capacity houses for productions of **Faith Healer**, **Death and the Maiden, Six Degrees of Separation**, **Oleanna, Hysteria, Cavalcaders, The Kitchen, The Queen & I, The Libertine, Simpatico, Mojo** and **The Steward of Christendom**.

Death and the Maiden and **Six Degrees of Separation** won the Olivier Award for Best Play in 1992 and 1993 respectively. **Hysteria** won the 1994 Olivier Award for Best Comedy, and also the Writers' Guild Award for Best West End Play. **My Night with Reg** won the 1994 Writers' Guild Award for Best Fringe Play, the Evening Standard Award for Best Comedy, and the 1994 Olivier Award for Best Comedy. Jonathan Harvey won the 1994 Evening Standard Drama Award for Most Promising Playwright, for **Babies**. Sebastian Barry won the 1995 Writers' Guild Award for Best Fringe Play for **The Steward of Christendom** and also the 1995 Lloyds Private Banking Playwright of the Year Award. Jez Butterworth won the 1995 George Devine Award for Most Promising Playwright, the 1995 Writers' Guild New Writer of the Year, the Evening Standard Award for Most Promising Newcomer and the 1995 Olivier Award for Best Comedy for **Mojo**. Phyllis Nagy won the 1995 Writers' Guild Award for Best Regional Play for **Disappeared**. Martin McDonagh won the 1996 George Devine Award for Most Promising Playwright, the 1996 Writers' Guild Best Fringe Play Award, and the 1996 Evening Standard Drama Award for Most Promising Newcomer for **The Beauty Queen of Leenane**. The Royal Court won the 1995 Prudential Award for the Theatre, and was the overall winner of the 1995 Prudential Award for the Arts for creativity, excellence, innovation and accessibility. The Royal Court won the 1995 Peter Brook Empty Space Award for innovation and excellence in theatre.

Now in its temporary homes The Duke Of York's and Ambassadors Theatres, during the two-year refurbishment of its Sloane Square theatre, the Royal Court continues to present the best in new work. After four decades the company's aims remain consistent with those established by George Devine. The Royal Court is still a major focus in the country for the production of new work. Scores of plays first seen at the Royal Court are now part of the national and international dramatic repertoire.

Druid Theatre Company

Druid Theatre Company was founded in 1975 by Garry Hynes, Mick Lally and Marie Mullen. Based in Galway, a growing city on the west coast of Ireland, and working from a theatre that seated 47 people, within a few years the company had evolved an ambitious repertoire and a dynamic style of the utmost professionalism.

The fact that Druid worked outside the theatrical mainstream (for many years it was the only professional theatre company in Ireland outside Dublin), allied with the pressure of the individual talents of its members, forced the company into a highly individual approach to all aspects of theatre. A distinctive style began to emerge particulary in the work of the company's leading actors including Marie Mullen, Sean McGinley, Maelíosa Stafford and Ray McBride and the work of artistic director Garry Hynes.

In 1983 the company began an association with one of Ireland's leading writers, Tom Murphy, and productions included **Conversations on a Homecoming,** and **Bailegangaire** with Siobhan McKenna. Both of these productions were seen in London at the Donmar Warehouse along with Druid's acclaimed production of **The Playboy of the Western World**. In the late eighties the company toured internationally with visits to New York and Sydney as well as regular UK dates including Glasgow and London.

In 1990 Garry Hynes left the company to become Artistic Director of the Abbey Theatre and Maelíosa Stafford was appointed to succeed her. Under Mr Stafford's direction the company began a policy of nurturing young writers and successes included Vincent Woods' **At the Black Pig's Dyke** and **Song of the Yellow Bittern. At The Black Pig's Dyke** was seen in London and Toronto in 1993/94 and was the centrepiece of the Sydney Festival in January 1995.

In October 1994 Garry Hynes returned as Artistic Director and began developing a comprehensive programme of new work. **The Beauty Queen of Leenane** opened the Town Hall Theatre, Galway on 1 February 1996 and marked the stage debut of Martin McDonagh. Other writers under commission to Druid include Billy Roche, Marina Carr, Niall Williams and Frank McGuinness.

In late 1996 as well as playing the Royal Court Downstairs, **The Beauty Queen of Leenane** toured some of the most westerly communities in Europe including seven islands ranging from Oileán Chléire in West Cork to Rathlin Island in Antrim. 1996 also saw Druid celebrate its 21st birthday with a production of Brian Friel's **The Loves of Cass Maguire.**

In 1998 Druid will produce all of Synge's plays in repertoire under the title **A Story Told Forever.** This project will premiere on Inis Meáin in late May 1998 marking the centenary of the playwright's first visit to the the island.

For Druid Theatre Company

Artistic Director **Garry Hynes**
General Manager **Louise Donlon**
Production Manager **Maurice Power**
Administrator **Maria Fleming**
Executive Assistant **Eoin Brady**
Casting **Maureen Hughes**

Druid Theatre Company
Druid Lane
Galway
Ireland
Telephone Box Office:
00 353 91 568617
Administration: 00 353 91 568660
Fax: 00 353 91 563109
email: druid@iol.ie

The Cripple of Inishmaan
a new play by Martin McDonagh

Auntie Eileen &
Auntie Kate

Cripple Billy

Mammy

Slippy Helen

Bartley

Johnnypateenmike

Photos: Gautier Deblonde

NT Royal
National
Theatre

In repertoire in the Lyttelton until 19 August

Box Office 0171-928 2252
First Call 0171-420 0000

Reg'd Charity

The Beauty Queen of Leenane

by Martin McDonagh

Cast

Mag Folan	Anna Manahan
Maureen Folan	Marie Mullen
Ray Dooley	Aidan McArdle
Pato Dooley	Brían F. O'Byrne

Director	Garry Hynes
Designer	Francis O'Connor
Lighting Designer	Ben Ormerod
Sound Design	Bell Helicopter
Music	Paddy Cunneen
Production Managers	Ed Wilson (RCT)
	Maurice Power (Druid)
Assistant Production Manager	Mark Townsend (RCT)
Design/Construction Consultant	James Probert
Company Stage Manager	Maris Sharp (RCT)
Company Stage Manager	Mairéad McGrath (Druid)
Deputy Stage Manager	Sophie Gabszewicz
Druid Handover Stage Management Team	Bernie Walsh & Niall Cranney
Costume Supervisor	Orfhlaith Stafford
Production Photographs	Ivan Kyncl
Set Construction	Stage Surgeons Ltd, PL Parsons Ltd, Scott Fleary Ltd.
Scenic Artist	Paddy Hamilton
Special Effects/Prop Makers	Mac Teo, Paula Conroy, Aquality

Special thanks to: Martin Riley, Lizz Poulter, Alan Clarke, the Town Hall Theatre, Galway and Druid Theatre Company production team.

The Beauty Queen of Leenane was originally produced with support from The Jerwood Foundation.

The Royal Court would like to thank the following for their help with this production: Auditorium redesign by Ultz; auditorium ceiling constructed by Stage Surgeons Ltd (0171 237 2765), rigged and suspended by Vertigo Rigging Ltd; Wardrobe care by Persil and Comfort courtesy of Lever Brothers Ltd, refrigerators by Electrolux and Philips Major Appliances Ltd.; kettles for rehearsals by Morphy Richards; video for casting purposes by Hitachi; backstage coffee machine by West 9; furniture by Knoll International; freezer for backstage use supplied by Zanussi Ltd 'Now that's a good idea.' Hair styling by Carole at Moreno, 2 Holbein Place, Sloane Square 0171- 730- 0211; Closed circuit TV cameras and monitors by Mitsubishi UK Ltd. Natural spring water from Aqua Cool, 12 Waterside Way, London SW17 0XH, tel. 0181-947 5666. Overhead projector from W.H. Smith; Sanyo U.K for the backstage microwave.

Martin McDonagh (writer)

For the Royal Court: The Beauty Queen of Leenane (co-production with Druid).

Other theatre includes: The Banshees of Inisheer, The Lieutenant of Inishmore, The Maamturk Rifleman.

Paddy Cunneen (music)

For the Royal Court: The Leenane Trilogy (co-production with Druid), Portia Coughlan (& Abbey), The Treatment.

He is an Associate Director of Cheek By Jowl Theatre Company and has written music for all but one of the company's productions since 1988.

Other composition for theatre includes: Angels in America - parts 1 & 2; Peer Gynt, Fuente Ovejuna, The Birthday Party, The Recruiting Officer, Fair Ladies at Poem Cards, The Cripple of Inishmaan, The Sea, The Devil's Disciple, Blue Remembered Hills, Chips With Everything, Othello (RNT); The Alchemist, The Changeling, Richard III, The Painter of Dishonour (RSC); A Doll's House, Seagull (Abbey & Gate); Popcorn (Nottingham Playhouse).

As musical director: Sweeney Todd, A Little Night Music (RNT); Company - winner of Music Industry Award, Cabaret (Donmar Warehouse).

Composition for radio includes: Cymbeline, The Jew of Malta, Mr Wroe's Virgins, Burdalane, Henry IV - parts 1 & 2, Tamburlaine.

Film and television and film includes: The Pan Loaf, The Maitlands, Two Oranges and a Mango, You Drive Me, The Big Fish, Memory Man, Bite.

Bell Helicopter (sound design)

For the Royal Court: The Leenane Trilogy (co-production with Druid); The Lights Are on But Nobody's At Home.

Original music and sound designs include For theatre/dance: Mrs Sweeny, Hit and Run (Mint Theatre); Independent State (Cremorne Theatre Brisbane, The Playhouse Sydney Opera House); Revelations (Traverse, Waterman's Arts Centre); Urban Originals (Berlin New Music Festival); Departure Lounge (ICA). For film: Irene is Not Herself Anymore, Les Vampires, You Don't Say,

Chocolate Acrobat, Mumford Diaries, Cities of Brick. For radio: Radio Works (Radio Granuille, Marseilles).

Installations include: Lines of Thought (Project Arts / La Friche); Statue and Other Moving Things (Project Arts Centre); Evening Echoes (Tour); The Width, Thickness and Viscosity of Ghosts (Spitalfields Public Toilets); Absence (Whitechapel Art Gallery); Walking (Nose Paint, London); Eye Witness (Endeavor House).

Garry Hynes (director)

Founded Druid Theatre Company in 1975. Artistic Director 1975-1991 and again from 1995 to date. Artistic Director of the Abbey Theatre, Dublin 1991-1994.

For the Royal Court: Portia Coughlan (& Abbey), A Whistle in the Dark (& Abbey); The Beauty Queen of Leenane (co-produced with Druid).

Other theatre includes: The Loves of Cass MacGuire, The Playboy of the Western World, Bailegangaire, Conversations on a Homecoming, Wood of the Whispering, 'Tis A Pity She's A Whore, Poor Beast in the Rain (Druid); King of the Castle, The Plough and the Stars, The Power of Darkness, Famine (Abbey); The Man of Mode, Song of the Nightingale (RSC); The Colleen Bawn (Royal Exchange Manchester). She is an Associate Director at the Royal Court.

Anna Manahan

For the Royal Court: Live Like Pigs, The Beauty Queen of Leenane (co-production with Druid).

Other theatre includes: The Loves of Cass MacGuire, I Do Not Like Thee, Dr. Fell (Druid); Lovers (London and USA, nomination Tony Award); The Shaughraun (Abbey); The Matchmaker, The Streets of Dublin (Tivoli); The Tailor and Ansty (Andrews Lane / Tivoli); The Guernica Hotel, Happy Birthday Dear Alice, The Crucible, The Old Lady's Guide to Survival (Red Kettle).

Anna worked extensively with the Edwards MacLiammoir Company, The Gate Theatre and all the major Irish companies, as well as Phyllis Ryan and Gemini Productions and the Royal National Theatre.

Film and television includes: The Bill, Lovejoy, The Young Indiana Jones Chronicles, The

Treaty, Blind Justice, A Man of No Importance, Hear My Song, The Irish RM, Me Mammy.

Aidan McArdle

For the Royal Court: Storming (Young Writers' Festival 1996).

Other theatre includes: Flight into Egypt (Hampstead); Boccaccio's Decameron (Gate); The Hamlet Project, The Last Apache Reunion, The Honeyspike, Comedy of Errors, On the Inside, On the Outside, The Iceman Cometh (Abbey).

Television: As You Like It.

Marie Mullen

Founder member of Druid Theatre Company in 1975.

For the Royal Court: The Beauty Queen of Leenane (co-production with Druid), The Cavalcaders (& Peacock).

Other theatre includes: Silverlands, Lovers Meeting, The Colleen Bawn, The Shaughraun, A Doll's House, Much Ado About Nothing, The Playboy of the Western World, Bailegangaire, 'Tis a Pity She's a Whore, Famine (Druid); A Crucial Week in the Life of a Grocer's Assistant, Drama at Inish, The Power of Darkness, The Plough and the Stars (Abbey); The Man of Mode, Love of the Nightingale, Man Who Came to Dinner, King Lear (RSC).

Film and television includes: The Butcher Boy, The Van, Snakes and Ladders, The Disappearance of Finbarr, Circle of Friends, Family, Hear My Song.

Brian F. O'Byrne

For the Royal Court: The Beauty Queen of Leenane (co-production with Druid).

Other theatre includes: Good Evening Mr Collins (Peacock); Sharon's Grave (Gate); The Drum (Co-Motion); Hapgood (Lincoln Centre, New York); The Sisters Rosensweig (Barrymore, New York); Marking (Pure Orange, New York); Seconds Out (Public, New York); The Madam Macadam Travelling Theatre Company, Grandchild of Kings (The Irish Repertory Theatre Company, New York); Philadelphia Here I Come, Playboy of the Western World, The Drum, Angel (Pedal Crank, New York); A Thousand Hours of Love (Theatre for New City, New York); The Country Boy, Moll (Irish Theatre Company, Buffalo).

Film includes: The Last Bus Home, The Fifth Province, Avenue X.

Francis O'Connor (designer)

For the Royal Court: The Beauty Queen of Leenane (co-production with Druid).

Other design for theatre includes: Wild Harvest (Druid); Tarry Flynn, The Importance of Being Earnest, She Stoops to Folly, Silverlands (Abbey); The Bread Man (Gate); All in the Timing, Aladdin, Dick Whittington (Nottingham Playhouse); The Clearing (Bush); After Easter (RSC); Sing to the Dawn, Little Shop of Horrors, Into the Woods (Singapore); Moby Dick (Germany); The Ugly Duckling (Watermill); Annie (Crucible).

Design for opera includes: Arladne Auf Naxos (Castleward); Linda Di Chamounix (Guildhall); May Night (Wexford Festival); La Vie Parisienne (D'Oyly Carte); The Barber of Seville (English Touring Opera); Rape of Lucretia (Guildhall); The Pirates of Penzance (Cleveland Theatre Company); La Boheme (Stowe Opera).

Future projects include: Enter the Guardsman (Donmar Warehouse); Love on the Throne (Nottingham Playhouse).

Ben Ormerod (lighting designer)

For the Royal Court: The Beauty Queen of Leenane (co-production with Druid).

Other lighting design for theatre includes: Uncle Vanya, Accidental Death of an Anarchist, Bent, The Winter's Tale (RNT); Hamlet, Twelfth Night, Comic Mysteries (Oxford Stage Company); Hedda Gabler, Hamlet (English Touring Theatre, Donmar Warehouse); Oedipus Rex (Epidaurus); Passing Places (Traverse); The House of Bernarda Alba (Theatre Clwyd).

Lighting design for opera includes: Il Trovatore (Scottish Opera); The Mask of Orpheus (Royal Festival Hall); The Cunning Peasant (Guildhall); Baa Baa Black Sheep (Opera North & BBC2).

Future productions include; All's Well That Ends Well (Oxford Stage Company); The Seagull (English Touring Theatre / Donmar Warehouse); A Time and a Season (Theatre Royal, Plymouth).

For the Royal Court

The Beauty Queen of Leenane

The Beauty Queen of Leenane, a Druid Theatre Company/Royal Court Theatre co-production, was first presented at the Town Hall Theatre, Galway, on 1st February 1996, marking the official opening of the theatre, and subsequently opened at the Royal Court Theatre Upstairs on 5th March 1996. The cast was as follows:

Mag	Anna Manahan
Maureen	Marie Mullen
Ray	Tom Murphy
Pato	Brían F. O'Byrne

Directed by Garry Hynes
Designed by Francis O'Connor
Lighting designed by Ben Ormerod
Sound by David Murphy

Characters

Maureen Folan, *aged forty. Plain, slim.*
Mag Folan, *her mother, aged seventy. Stout, frail.*
Pato Dooley, *a good-looking local man, aged about forty.*
Ray Dooley, *his brother, aged twenty.*

Setting: Leenane, a small town in Connemara, County Galway.

Scene One

The living-room/kitchen of a rural cottage in the west of Ireland. Front door stage left, a long black range along the back wall with a box of turf beside it and a rocking-chair on its right. On the kitchen side of the set is a door in the back wall leading off to an unseen hallway, and a newer oven, a sink and some cupboards curving around the right wall. There is a window with an inner ledge above the sink in the right wall looking out onto fields, a dinner table with two chairs just right of centre, a small TV down left, an electric kettle and a radio on one of the kitchen cupboards, a crucifix and a framed picture of John and Robert Kennedy on the wall above the range, a heavy black poker beside the range, and a touristy-looking embroidered tea-towel hanging further along the back wall, bearing the inscription 'May you be half an hour in Heaven afore the Devil knows you're dead'. As the play begins it is raining quite heavily.
Mag Folan, *a stoutish woman in her early seventies with short, tightly permed grey hair and a mouth that gapes slightly, is sitting in the rocking-chair, staring off into space. Her left hand is somewhat more shrivelled and red than her right. The front door opens and her daughter,* **Maureen**, *a plain, slim woman of about forty, enters carrying shopping and goes through to the kitchen.*

Mag Wet, Maureen?

Maureen Of course wet.

Mag Oh-h.

Maureen *takes her coat off, sighing, and starts putting the shopping away.*

Mag I did take me Complan.

Maureen So you *can* get it yourself so.

Mag I can. (*Pause.*) Although lumpy it was, Maureen.

Maureen Well, can I help lumpy?

Mag No.

Maureen Write to the Complan people so, if it's lumpy.

Mag (*pause*) You do make me Complan nice and smooth. (*Pause.*) Not a lump at all, nor the comrade of a lump.

Maureen   You don't give it a good enough stir is what you don't do.

Mag   I gave it a good enough stir and there was still lumps.

Maureen   You probably pour the water in too fast so. What it says on the box, you're supposed to ease it in.

Mag   Mm.

Maureen   That's where you do go wrong. Have another go tonight for yourself and you'll see.

Mag   Mm. (*Pause.*) And the hot water too I do be scared of. Scared I may scould meself.

Maureen *gives her a slight look.*

Mag   I *do* be scared, Maureen. I be scared what if me hand shook and I was to pour it over me hand. And with you at Mary Pender's, then where would I be?

Maureen   You're just a hypochondriac is what you are.

Mag   I'd be lying on the floor and I'm not a hypochondriac.

Maureen   You are too and everybody knows that you are. Full well.

Mag   Don't I have a urine infection if I'm such a hypochondriac?

Maureen   I can't see how a urine infection prevents you pouring a mug of Complan or tidying up the house a bit when I'm away. It wouldn't kill you.

Mag (*pause*)   Me bad back.

Maureen   Your bad back.

Mag   And me bad hand. (**Mag** *holds up her shrivelled hand for a second.*)

Maureen (*quietly*)   Feck ... (*Irritated.*) I'll get your Complan so if it's such a big job! From now and 'til doomsday! The one thing I ask you to do. Do you see Annette or Margo coming pouring your Complan or buying your oul cod in butter sauce for the week?

Mag   No.

Maureen   No is right, you don't. And carrying it up that hill. And still I'm not appreciated.

Mag   You *are* appreciated, Maureen.

Maureen   I'm not appreciated.

Mag   I'll give me Complan another go so, and give it a good stir for meself.

Maureen   Ah, forget your Complan. I'm expected to do everything else, I suppose that one on top of it won't hurt. Just a . . . just a blessed fecking skivvy is all I'm thought of!

Mag   You're not, Maureen.

Maureen *slams a couple of cupboard doors after finishing with the shopping and sits at the table, after dragging its chair back loudly. Pause.*

Mag   Me porridge, Maureen, I haven't had, will you be getting? No, in a minute, Maureen, have a rest for yourself . . .

But **Maureen** *has already jumped up, stomped angrily back to the kitchen and started preparing the porridge as noisily as she can. Pause.*

Mag   Will we have the radio on for ourselves?

Maureen *bangs an angry finger at the radio's 'on' switch. It takes a couple of swipes before it comes on loudly, through static – a nasally male voice singing in Gaelic. Pause.*

Mag   The dedication Annette and Margo sent we still haven't heard. I wonder what's keeping it?

Maureen   If they sent a dedication at all. They only said they did. (**Maureen** *sniffs the sink a little, then turns to* **Mag**.) Is there a smell off this sink now, I'm wondering.

Mag (*defensively*)   No.

Maureen   I hope there's not, now.

Mag   No smell at all is there, Maureen. I do promise, now.

Maureen *returns to the porridge. Pause.*

Mag   Is the radio a biteen loud there, Maureen?

Maureen   A biteen loud, is it?

Maureen *swipes angrily at the radio again, turning it off. Pause.*

Mag   Nothing on it, anyways. An oul fella singing nonsense.

Maureen   Isn't it you wanted it set for that oul station?

Mag   Only for Ceilidh Time and for whatyoucall.

Maureen   It's too late to go complaining now.

Mag   Not for nonsense did I want it set.

Maureen (*pause*)   It isn't nonsense anyways. Isn't it Irish?

Mag   It sounds like nonsense to me. Why can't they just speak English like everybody?

Maureen   Why should they speak English?

Mag   To know what they're saying.

Maureen   What country are you living in?

Mag   Eh?

Maureen   What country are you living in?

Mag   Galway.

Maureen   Not what county!

Mag   Oh-h . . .

Maureen   Ireland you're living in!

Mag   *Ireland.*

Maureen   So why should you be speaking English in Ireland?

Mag   I don't know why.

Maureen   It's Irish you should be speaking in Ireland.

Mag   It is.

Maureen   Eh?

Mag   Eh?

Maureen 'Speaking English in Ireland.'

Mag (*pause*) Except where would Irish get you going for a job in England? Nowhere.

Maureen Well, isn't that the crux of the matter?

Mag Is it, Maureen?

Maureen If it wasn't for the English stealing our language, and our land, and our God-knows-what, wouldn't it be we wouldn't need to go over there begging for jobs and for handouts?

Mag I suppose that's the crux of the matter.

Maureen It *is* the crux of the matter.

Mag (*pause*) Except America, too.

Maureen What except America too?

Mag If it was to America you had to go begging for handouts, it isn't Irish would be any good to you. It would be English!

Maureen Isn't that the same crux of the same matter?

Mag I don't know if it is or it isn't.

Maureen Bringing up kids to think all they'll ever be good for is begging handouts from the English and the Yanks. That's the selfsame crux.

Mag I suppose.

Maureen Of course you suppose, because it's true.

Mag (*pause*) If I had to go begging for handouts anywhere, I'd rather beg for them in America than in England, because in America it does be more sunny anyways. (*Pause.*) Or is that just something they say, that the weather is more sunny, Maureen? Or is that a lie, now?

Maureen *slops the porridge out and hands it to* **Mag**, *speaking as she does so.*

Maureen   You're oul and you're stupid and you don't know what you're talking about. Now shut up and eat your oul porridge.

Maureen *goes back to wash the pan in the sink.* **Mag** *glances at the porridge, then turns back to her.*

Mag   Me mug of tea you forgot!

Maureen *clutches the edges of the sink and lowers her head, exasperated, then quietly, with visible self-control, fills the kettle to make her mother's tea. Pause.* **Mag** *speaks while slowly eating.*

Mag   Did you meet anybody on your travels, Maureen? (*No response.*) Ah no, not on a day like today. (*Pause.*) Although you don't say hello to people is your trouble, Maureen. (*Pause.*) Although some people it would be better not to say hello to. The fella up and murdered the poor oul woman in Dublin and he didn't even know her. The news that story was on, did you hear of it? (*Pause.*) Strangled, and didn't even know her. That's a fella it would be better not to talk to. That's a fella it would be better to avoid outright.

Maureen *brings* **Mag** *her tea, then sits at the table.*

Maureen   Sure, that sounds exactly the type of fella I would *like* to meet, and then bring him home to meet you, if he likes murdering oul women.

Mag   That's not a nice thing to say, Maureen.

Maureen   Is it not, now?

Mag (*pause*)   Sure why would he be coming all this way out from Dublin? He'd just be going out of his way.

Maureen   For the pleasure of me company he'd come. Killing you, it'd just be a bonus for him.

Mag   Killing *you* I bet he first would be.

Maureen   I could live with that so long as I was sure he'd be clobbering you soon after. If he clobbered you with a big axe or something and took your oul head off and spat in your neck, I wouldn't mind at all, going first. Oh no, I'd enjoy it, I would.

No more oul Complan to get, and no more oul porridge to get, and no more . . .

Mag (*interrupting, holding her tea out*)   No sugar in this, Maureen, you forgot, go and get me some.

Maureen *stares at her a moment, then takes the tea, brings it to the sink and pours it away, goes back to* **Mag***, grabs her half-eaten porridge, returns to the kitchen, scrapes it out into the bin, leaves the bowl in the sink and exits into the hallway, giving* **Mag** *a dirty look on the way and closing the door behind her.* **Mag** *stares grumpily out into space. Blackout.*

Scene Two

Mag *is sitting at the table, staring at her reflection in a hand-mirror. She pats her hair a couple of times. The TV is on, showing an old episode of* The Sullivans. *There is a knock at the front door, which startles her slightly.*

Mag   Who . . . ? Maureen. Oh-h. The door, Maureen.

Mag *gets up and shuffles towards the kitchen window. There is another knock. She shuffles back to the door.*

Who's at the door?

Ray (*off*)   It's Ray Dooley, Mrs. From over the way.

Mag   Dooley?

Ray   Ray Dooley, aye. You know me.

Mag   Are you one of the Dooleys so?

Ray   I am. I'm Ray.

Mag   Oh-h.

Ray (*pause. Irritated*)   Well, will you let me in or am I going to talk to the door?

Mag   She's feeding the chickens. (*Pause.*) Have you gone?

Ray (*angrily*)   Open the oul door, Mrs! Haven't I walked a mile out of me way just to get here?

Mag   Have you?

Ray   I have. 'Have you?' she says.

Mag *unlatches the door with some difficulty and* **Ray Dooley**, *a lad of about nineteen, enters.*

Ray   Thank you! An hour I thought you'd be keeping me waiting.

Mag   Oh, it's you, so it is.

Ray   Of course it's me. Who else?

Mag   You're the Dooley with the uncle.

Ray   It's only a million times you've seen me the past twenty year. Aye, I'm the Dooley with the uncle, and it's me uncle the message is.

Ray *stops and watches the TV a moment.*

Mag   Maureen's at the chickens.

Ray   You've said Maureen's at the chickens. What's on the telly?

Mag   I was waiting for the news.

Ray   You'll have a long wait.

Mag   I was combing me hair.

Ray   I think it's *The Sullivans*.

Mag   I don't know what it is.

Ray   You do get a good reception.

Mag   A middling reception.

Ray   Everything's Australian nowadays.

Mag   I don't know if it is or it isn't.

Mag *sits in the rocking-chair.*

At the chickens, Maureen is.

Ray   That's three times now you've told me Maureen's at the chickens. Are you going for the world's record in saying 'Maureen's at the chickens'?

Mag (*pause. Confused*)   She's feeding them.

Ray *stares at her a moment, then sighs and looks out through the kitchen window.*

Ray   Well, I'm not wading through all that skitter just to tell her. I've done enough wading. Coming up that oul hill.

Mag   It's a big oul hill.

Ray   It *is* a big oul hill.

Mag   Steep.

Ray   Steep is right and if not steep then muddy.

Mag   Muddy and rocky.

Ray   Muddy and rocky is right. Uh-huh. How do ye two manage up it every day?

Mag   We do drive.

Ray   Of course. (*Pause.*) That's what I want to do is drive. I'll have to be getting driving lessons. And a car. (*Pause.*) Not a good one, like. A second-hand one, y'know?

Mag   A used one.

Ray   A used one, aye.

Mag   Off somebody.

Ray   Oul Father Welsh – Walsh – has a car he's selling, but I'd look a poof buying a car off a priest.

Mag   I don't like Father Walsh – Welsh – at all.

Ray   He punched Mairtin Hanlon in the head once, and for no reason.

Mag   God love us!

Ray   Aye. Although, now, that was out of character for Father Welsh. Father Welsh seldom uses violence, same as most young priests. It's usually only the older priests go punching you in the head. I don't know why. I suppose it's the way they were brought up.

Mag   There was a priest the news Wednesday had a babby with a Yank!

Ray   That's no news at all. That's everyday. It'd be hard to find a priest who hasn't had a babby with a Yank. If he'd punched that babby in the head, that'd be news. Aye. Anyways. Aye. What was I saying? Oh aye, so if I give you the message, Mrs, you'll be passing it on to Maureen, so you will, or will I be writing it down for you?

Mag   I'll be passing it on.

Ray   Good-oh. Me brother Pato said to invite yous to our uncle's going-away do. The Riordan's hall out in Carraroe.

Mag   Is your brother back so?

Ray   He is.

Mag   Back from England?

Ray   Back from England, aye. England's where he was, so that's where he would be back from. Our Yankee uncle's going home to Boston after his holiday and taking those two ugly duckling daughters back with him and that Dolores whatyoucall, Healey or Hooley, so there'll be a little to-do in the Riordan's as a goodbye or a *big* to-do knowing them show-off bastards and free food anyways, so me brother says ye're welcome to come or Maureen anyways, he knows you don't like getting out much. Isn't it you has the bad hip?

Mag   No.

Ray   Oh. Who is it has the bad hip so?

Mag   I don't know. I do have the urine infection.

Ray   Maybe that's what I was thinking of. And thanks for telling me.

Mag   Me urine.

Ray   I know, your urine.

Mag   And me bad back. And me burned hand.

Ray   Aye, aye, aye. Anyways, you'll be passing the message on to that one.

Mag   Eh?

Ray   You'll be remembering the message to pass it on to that one?

Mag   Aye.

Ray   Say it back to me so.

Mag   Say it back to you?

Ray   Aye.

Mag (*long pause*)   Me hip . . . ?

Ray (*angrily*)   I should've fecking written it down in the first fecking place, I fecking knew! And save all this fecking time!

Ray *grabs a pen and a piece of paper, sits at the table and writes the message out.*

Talking with a loon!

Mag (*pause*)   Do me a mug of tea while you're here, Pato. Em, Ray.

Ray   *Ray* my fecking name is! Pato's me fecking brother!

Mag   I do forget.

Ray   It's like talking to a . . . talking to a . . .

Mag   Brick wall.

Ray   Brick wall is right.

Mag (*pause*)   Or some soup do me.

Ray *finishes writing and gets up.*

Ray   There. Forget about soup. The message is there. Point that one in the direction of it when she returns from beyond. The Riordan's hall out in Carraroe. Seven o'clock tomorrow night. Free food. Okay?

Mag   All right now, Ray. Are you still in the choir nowadays, Ray?

Ray   I am *not* in the choir nowadays. Isn't it ten years since I was in the choir?

Mag   Doesn't time be flying?

Ray   Not since I took an interest in girls have I been in the choir because you do get no girls in choirs, only fat girls and what use are they? No. I go to discos, me.

Mag   Good enough for yourself.

Ray   What am I doing standing around here conversing with you? I have left me message and now I am off.

Mag   Goodbye to you, Ray.

Ray   Goodbye to you, Mrs.

Mag   And pull the door.

Ray   I was going to pull the door anyways . . .

Ray pulls the front door shut behind him as he exits.

(*Off.*) I don't need your advice!

As **Ray**'s *footsteps fade,* **Mag** *gets up, reads the message on the table, goes to the kitchen window and glances out, then finds a box of matches, comes back to the table, strikes a match, lights the message, goes to the range with it burning and drops it inside. Sound of footsteps approaching the front door.* **Mag** *shuffles back to her rocking chair and sits in it just as* **Maureen** *enters.*

Mag (*nervously*)   Cold, Maureen?

Maureen   Of course cold.

Mag   Oh-h.

Mag *stares at the TV as if engrossed.* **Maureen** *sniffs the air a little, then sits at the table, staring at* **Mag**.

Maureen   What are you watching?

Mag   I don't know *what* I'm watching. Just waiting for the news I am.

Maureen   Oh aye. (*Pause.*) Nobody rang while I was out, I suppose? Ah no.

Mag   Ah no, Maureen. Nobody did ring.

Maureen   Ah no.

Mag   No. Who would be ringing?

Maureen   No, nobody I suppose. No. (*Pause.*) And nobody visited us either? Ah no.

Mag   Ah no, Maureen. Who would be visiting us?

Maureen   Nobody, I suppose. Ah no.

Mag *glances at* **Maureen** *a second, then back at the TV. Pause.*
Maureen *gets up, ambles over to the TV, lazily switches it off with the toe of her shoe, ambles back to the kitchen, staring at* **Mag** *as she passes, turns on the kettle, and leans against the cupboards, looking back in* **Mag**'*s direction.*

Mag (*nervously*)   Em, apart from wee Ray Dooley who passed.

Maureen (*knowing*)   Oh, did Ray Dooley pass, now?

Mag   He passed, aye, and said hello as he was passing.

Maureen   I thought just now you said there was no visitors.

Mag   There was no visitors, no, apart from Ray Dooley who passed.

Maureen   Oh, aye, aye, aye. Just to say hello he popped his head in.

Mag   Just to say hello and how is all. Aye. A nice wee lad he is.

Maureen   Aye. (*Pause.*) With no news?

Mag   With no news. Sure, what news would a gasur have?

Maureen   None at all, I suppose. Ah, no.

Mag   Ah, no. (*Pause.*) Thinking of getting a car I think he said he was.

Maureen   Oh aye?

Mag   A second-hand one.

Maureen   Uh-huh?

Mag   To drive, y'know?

Maureen   To drive, aye.

Mag   Off Father Welsh – Walsh – Welsh.

Maureen   Welsh.

Mag   Welsh.

Maureen *switches off the kettle, pours a sachet of Complan into a mug and fills it up with water.*

Maureen   I'll do you some of your Complan.

Mag   Have I not had me Complan already, Maureen? I have.

Maureen   Sure, another one won't hurt.

Mag (*wary*)   No, I suppose.

Maureen *tops the drink up with tap water to cool it, stirs it just twice to keep it lumpy, takes the spoon out, hands the drink to* **Mag**, *then leans back against the table to watch her drink it.* **Mag** *looks at it in distaste.*

Mag   A bit lumpy, Maureen.

Maureen   Never mind lumpy, mam. The lumps will do you good. That's the best part of Complan is the lumps. Drink ahead.

Mag   A little spoon, do you have?

Maureen   No, I have no little spoon. There's no little spoons for liars in this house. No little spoons at all. Be drinking ahead.

Mag *takes the smallest of sickly sips.*

Maureen   The whole of it, now!

Mag   I do have a funny tummy, Maureen, and I do have no room.

Maureen   Drink ahead, I said! You had room enough to be spouting your lies about Ray Dooley had no message! Did I not meet him on the road beyond as he was going? The lies of you. The whole of that Complan you'll drink now, and suck the lumps down too, and whatever's left you haven't drank, it is over your head I will be emptying it, and you know well enough I mean it!

Mag *slowly drinks the rest of the sickly brew.*

Maureen Arsing me around, eh? Interfering with my life again? Isn't it enough I've had to be on beck and call for you every day for the past twenty year? Is it one evening out you begrudge me?

Mag Young girls should not be out gallivanting with fellas . . . !

Maureen Young girls! I'm forty years old, for feck's sake! Finish it!

Mag *drinks again.*

Maureen 'Young girls'! That's the best yet. And how did Annette or Margo ever get married if it wasn't first out gallivanting that they were?

Mag I don't know.

Maureen Drink!

Mag I don't like it, Maureen.

Maureen Would you like it better over your head?

Mag *drinks again.*

Maureen I'll tell you, eh? 'Young girls out gallivanting.' I've heard it all now. What have I ever done but *kissed* two men the past forty year?

Mag Two men is plenty!

Maureen Finish!

Mag I've finished!

Mag *holds out the mug.* **Maureen** *washes it.*

Two men is two men too much!

Maureen To you, maybe. To you. Not to me.

Mag Two men too much!

Maureen Do you think I like being stuck up here with you? Eh? Like a dried up oul . . .

Mag Whore!

Maureen *laughs.*

Maureen 'Whore'? (*Pause.*) Do I not *wish*, now? Do I not wish? (*Pause.*) Sometimes I *dream* . . .

Mag Of being a . . . ?

Maureen Of anything! (*Pause. Quietly.*) Of anything. Other than this.

Mag Well an odd dream that is!

Maureen It's not at all. Not at all is it an odd dream. (*Pause.*) And if it is it's not the only odd dream I do have. Do you want to be hearing another one?

Mag I don't.

Maureen I have a dream sometimes there of you, dressed all nice and white, in your coffin there, and me all in black looking in on you, and a fella beside me there, comforting me, the smell of aftershave off him, his arm round me waist. And the fella asks me then if I'll be going for a drink with him at his place after.

Mag And what do you say?

Maureen I say 'Aye, what's stopping me now?'

Mag You don't!

Maureen I do!

Mag At me funeral?

Maureen At your bloody wake, sure! Is even sooner!

Mag Well that's not a nice thing to be dreaming!

Maureen I know it's not, sure, and it isn't a *dream*-dream at all. It's more of a day-dream. Y'know, something happy to be thinking of when I'm scraping the skitter out of them hens.

Mag Not at all is that a nice dream. That's a mean dream.

Maureen I don't know if it is or it isn't.

Pause. **Maureen** *sits at the table with a pack of Kimberley biscuits.*

I suppose now you'll never be dying. You'll be hanging on forever, just to spite me.

Mag   I *will* be hanging on forever!

Maureen   I know well you will!

Mag   Seventy you'll be at my wake, and then how many men'll there be round your waist with their aftershave?

Maureen   None at all, I suppose.

Mag   None at all is right!

Maureen   Oh aye. (*Pause.*) Do you want a Kimberley?

Mag (*pause*)   Have we no shortbread fingers?

Maureen   No, you've ate all the shortbread fingers. Like a pig.

Mag   I'll have a Kimberley so, although I don't like Kimberleys. I don't know why you get Kimberleys at all. Kimberleys are horrible.

Maureen   Me world doesn't revolve around your taste in biscuits.

Maureen *gives* **Mag** *a biscuit.* **Mag** *eats.*

Mag (*pause*)   You'll be going to this do tomorrow so?

Maureen   I will. (*Pause.*) It'll be good to see Pato again anyways. I didn't even know he was home.

Mag   But it's all them oul Yanks'll be there tomorrow.

Maureen   So?

Mag   You said you couldn't stand the Yanks yesterday. The crux of the matter yesterday you said it was.

Maureen   Well, I suppose now, mother, I will have to be changing me mind, but, sure, isn't that a woman's prerogative?

Mag (*quietly*)   It's only prerogatives when it suits you.

Maureen   Don't go using big words you don't understand, now, mam.

Mag (*sneers. Pause*)   This invitation was open to me too, if you'd like to know.

Maureen (*half-laughing*)   Do you think you'll be coming?

Mag   I won't, I suppose.

Maureen   You suppose right enough. Lying the head off you, like the babby of a tinker.

Mag   I was only saying.

Maureen   Well, don't be saying. (*Pause.*) I think we might take a drive into Westport later, if it doesn't rain.

Mag (*brighter*)   Will we take a drive?

Maureen   We could take a little drive for ourselves.

Mag   We could now. It's a while since we did take a nice drive. We could get some shortbread fingers.

Maureen   Later on, I'm saying.

Mag   Later on. Not just now.

Maureen   Not just now. Sure, you've only just had your Complan now.

Mag *gives her a dirty look. Pause.*

Maureen   Aye, Westport. Aye. And I think I might pick up a nice little dress for meself while I'm there. For the do tomorrow, y'know?

Maureen *looks across at* **Mag**, *who looks back at her, irritated. Blackout.*

Scene Three

Night. Set only just illuminated by the orange coals through the bars of the range. Radio has been left on low in the kitchen. Footsteps and voices of **Maureen** *and* **Pato** *are heard outside, both slightly drunk.*

Pato (*off, singing*)   'The Cadillac stood by the house . . . '

Maureen (*off*)   Shh, Pato . . .

Pato (*off. Singing quietly*)   'And the Yanks they were within.' (*Speaking.*) What was it that oul fella used to say, now?

Maureen (*off*)   What oul fella, now?

Maureen *opens the door and the two of them enter, turning the lights on.* **Maureen** *is in a new black dress, cut quite short.* **Pato** *is a good-looking man of about the same age as her.*

Pato   The oul fella who used to chase oul whatyoucall. Oul Bugs Bunny.

Maureen   Would you like a cup of tea, Pato?

Pato   I would.

Maureen *switches the kettle on.*

Maureen   Except keep your voice down, now.

Pato (*quietly*)   I will, I will. (*Pause.*) I can't remember *what* he used to say. The oul fella used to chase Bugs Bunny. It was something, now.

Maureen   Look at this. The radio left on too, the daft oul bitch.

Pato   Sure, what harm? No, leave it on, now. It'll cover up the sounds.

Maureen   What sounds?

Pato   The smooching sounds.

He gently pulls her to him and they kiss a long while, then stop and look at each other. The kettle has boiled. **Maureen** *gently breaks away, smiling, and starts making the tea.*

Maureen   Will you have a biscuit with your tea?

Pato   I will. What biscuits do you have, now?

Maureen   Em, only Kimberleys.

Pato   I'll leave it so, Maureen. I do hate Kimberleys. In fact I think Kimberleys are the most horrible biscuits in the world.

Maureen   The same as that, I hate Kimberleys. I only get them to torment me mother.

Pato   I can't see why the Kimberley people go making them at all. Coleman Connor ate a whole pack of Kimberleys one time and he was sick for a week. (*Pause.*) Or was it Mikados? It was some kind of horrible biscuits.

Maureen   Is it true Coleman cut the ears off Valene's dog and keeps them in his room in a bag?

Pato   He showed me them ears one day.

Maureen   That's awful spiteful, cutting the ears off a dog.

Pato   It *is* awful spiteful.

Maureen   It would be spiteful enough to cut the ears off anybody's dog, let alone your own brother's dog.

Pato   And it had seemed a nice dog.

Maureen   Aye. (*Pause.*) Aye.

Awkward pause. **Pato** *cuddles up behind her.*

Pato   You feel nice to be giving a squeeze to.

Maureen   Do I?

Pato   Very nice.

Maureen *continues making the tea as* **Pato** *holds her. A little embarrassed and awkward, he breaks away from her after a second and idles a few feet away.*

Maureen   Be sitting down for yourself, now, Pato.

Pato   I will. (*Sits at table.*) I do do what I'm told, I do.

Maureen   Oh-ho, do you now? That's the first time tonight I did notice. Them stray oul hands of yours.

Pato   Sure, I have no control over me hands. They have a mind of their own. (*Pause.*) Except I didn't notice you complaining overmuch anyways, me stray oul hands. Not too many complaints at all!

Maureen   I had complaints when they were straying over that Yank girl earlier on in the evening.

Pato   Well, I hadn't noticed you there at that time, Maureen. How was I to know the beauty queen of Leenane was still yet to arrive?

Maureen 'The beauty queen of Leenane.' Get away with ya!

Pato Is true!

Maureen Why so have no more than two words passed between us the past twenty year?

Pato Sure, it's took me all this time to get up the courage.

Maureen (*smiling*) Ah, bollocks to ya!

Pato *smiles.* **Maureen** *brings the tea over and sits down.*

Pato I don't know, Maureen. I don't know.

Maureen Don't know what?

Pato Why I never got around to really speaking to you or asking you out or the like. I don't know. Of course, hopping across to that bastarding oul place every couple of months couldn't've helped.

Maureen England? Aye. Do you not like it there so?

Pato (*pause*) It's money. (*Pause.*) And it's Tuesday I'll be back there again.

Maureen Tuesday? This Tuesday?

Pato Aye. (*Pause.*) It was only to see the Yanks off I was over. To say hello and say goodbye. No time back at all.

Maureen That's Ireland, anyways. There's always someone leaving.

Pato It's always the way.

Maureen Bad, too.

Pato What can you do?

Maureen Stay?

Pato (*pause*) I do ask meself, if there was good work in Leenane, would I stay in Leenane? I mean, there never will be good work, but hypothetically, I'm saying. Or even bad work. Any work. And when I'm over there in London and working in rain and it's more or less cattle I am, and the young fellas cursing over cards and drunk and sick, and the oul digs over there, all pee-stained mattresses and nothing to do but watch the clock . . . when it's there I am, it's here I wish I was, of course. Who wouldn't? But when it's here I am . . . it isn't *there* I want to be, of course not. But I know it isn't here I want to be either.

Maureen   And why, Pato?

Pato   I can't put my finger on why. (*Pause.*) Of course it's beautiful here, a fool can see. The mountains and the green, and people speak. But when everybody knows everybody else's business . . . I don't know. (*Pause.*) You can't kick a cow in Leenane without some bastard holding a grudge twenty year.

Maureen   It's true enough.

Pato   It is. In England they don't care if you live or die, and it's funny but that isn't altogether a bad thing. Ah, sometimes it is . . . ah, I don't know.

Maureen (*pause*)   Do you think you'll ever settle down in the one place so, Pato? When you get married, I suppose.

Pato (*half-laughing*)   'When I get married . . . '

Maureen   You will someday, I'll bet you, get married. Wouldn't you want to?

Pato   I can't say it's something I do worry me head over.

Maureen   Of course, the rake of women you have stashed all over, you wouldn't need to.

Pato (*smiling*)   I have no rake of women.

Maureen   You have one or two, I bet.

Pato   I may have one or two. That I know to say hello to, now.

Maureen   Hello me . . . A-hole.

Pato   Is true. (*Pause.*) Sure, I'm no . . .

Maureen (*pause*)   No what?

Pause. **Pato** *shrugs and shakes his head, somewhat sadly. Pause. The song 'The Spinning Wheel', sung by Delia Murphy, has just started on the radio.*

Maureen (*continued*)   Me mother does love this oul song. Oul Delia Murphy.

Pato   This is a creepy oul song.

Maureen   It *is* a creepy oul song.

Pato   She does have a creepy oul voice. Always scared me this song did when I was a lad. She's like a ghoul singing. (*Pause.*) Does the grandmother die at the end, now, or is she just sleeping?

Maureen   Just sleeping, I think she is.

Pato   Aye...

Maureen (*pause*)   While the two go hand in hand through the fields.

Pato   Aye.

Maureen   Be moonlight.

Pato (*nods*)   They don't write songs like that any more. Thank Christ. (**Maureen** *laughs. Brighter.*) Wasn't it a grand night though, Maureen, now?

Maureen   It was.

Pato   Didn't we send them on their way well?

Maureen   We did, we did.

Pato   Not a dry eye.

Maureen   Indeed.

Pato   Eh?

Maureen   Indeed.

Pato   Aye. That we did. That we did.

Maureen (*pause*)   So who *was* the Yankee girl you did have your hands all over?

Pato (*laughing*)   Oh, will you stop it with your 'hands all over'?! Barely touched her, I did.

Maureen   Oh-ho!

Pato   A second cousin of me uncle, I think she is. Dolores somebody. Healey or Hooley. Healey. Boston, too, she lives.

Maureen   That was illegal so if it's your second cousin she is.

Pato   Illegal me arse, and it's not *my* second cousin she is anyway, and what's so illegal? Your second cousin's boobs aren't out of bounds, are they?

Maureen   They are!

Pato   I don't know about that. I'll have to consult with me lawyer on that one. I may get arrested the next time. And I have a defence anyways. She had dropped some Taytos on her blouse, there, I was just brushing them off for her.

Maureen   Taytos me arsehole, Pato Dooley!

Pato   Is true! (*Lustful pause. Nervously.*) Like this is all it was . . .

Pato *slowly reaches out and gently brushes at, then gradually fondles,* **Maureen**'s *breasts. She caresses his hand as he's doing so, then slowly gets up and sits across his lap, fondling his head as he continues touching her.*

Maureen   She was prettier than me.

Pato   You're pretty.

Maureen   She was prettier.

Pato   I like you.

Maureen   You have blue eyes.

Pato   I do.

Maureen   Stay with me tonight.

Pato   I don't know, now, Maureen.

Maureen   Stay. Just tonight.

Pato (*pause*)   Is your mother asleep?

Maureen   I don't care if she is or she isn't. (*Pause.*) Go lower.

Pato *begins easing his hands down her front.*

Maureen   Go lower ... Lower ...

His hands reach her crotch. She tilts her head back slightly. The song on the radio ends. Blackout.

Scene Four

Morning. **Maureen**'s *black dress is lying across the table.* **Mag** *enters from the hall carrying a potty of urine, which she pours out down the sink. She exits into the hall to put the potty away and returns a moment later, wiping her empty hands on the sides of her nightie. She spots the black dress and picks it up disdainfully.*

Mag   Forty pounds just for that skimpy dress? That dress is just skimpy. And laying it around then?

She tosses the dress into a far corner, returns to the kitchen and switches the kettle on, speaking loudly to wake **Maureen**.

I suppose I'll have to be getting me own Complan too, the hour you dragged yourself in whatever time it was with your oul dress. (*Quietly.*) That dress just looks silly. (*Loudly.*) Go the whole hog and wear no dress would be nearer the mark! (*Quietly.*) Snoring the head off you all night. Making an oul woman get her Complan, not to mention her porridge. Well, I won't be getting me own porridge, I'll tell you that now. I'd be afeard. You won't catch me getting me own porridge. Oh no. You won't be catching me out so easily.

Pato *has just entered from the hall, dressed in trousers and pulling on a shirt.*

Pato   Good morning there, now, Mrs.

Mag *is startled, staring at* **Pato** *dumbfounded.*

Mag   Good morning there, now.

Pato   Is it porridge you're after?

Mag   It is.

Pato   I'll be getting your porridge for you, so, if you like.

Mag   Oh-h.

Pato   Go ahead and rest yourself.

Mag *sits in the rocking chair, keeping her eyes on* **Pato** *all the while as he prepares her porridge.*

Pato   It's many the time I did get me brother his porridge of a school morning, so I'm well accustomed. (*Pause.*) You couldn't make it to the oul Yanks' do yesterday so?

Mag   No.

Pato   Your bad hip it was, Maureen was saying.

Mag (*still shocked*)   Aye, me bad hip. (*Pause.*) Where's Maureen, now?

Pato   Em, having a lie-in a minute or two, she is. (*Pause.*) To tell you the truth, I was all for . . . I was all for creeping out before ever you got yourself up, but Maureen said 'Aren't we all adults, now? What harm?' I suppose we are, but . . . I don't know. It's still awkward, now, or something. D'you know what I mean? I don't know. (*Pause.*) The Yanks'll be touching down in Boston about now anyways. God willing anyways. Aye. (*Pause.*) A good oul send-off we gave them anyways, we did, to send them off. Aye. (*Pause.*) Not a dry eye. (*Pause.*) Aye. (*Pause.*) Was it a mug of Complan too you wanted?

Mag   It was.

Pato *fixes her Complan and brings it over.*

Pato   You like your Complan so.

Mag   I don't.

Pato   Do you not, now?

Mag   She makes me drink it when I don't like it and forces me.

Pato   But Complan's good for you anyways if you're old.

Mag   I suppose it's good for me.

Pato   It is. Isn't it chicken flavour?

Mag   I don't know what flavour.

Pato (*checking box*)   Aye, it's chicken flavour. That's the best flavour.

Pato *returns to the porridge.*

Mag (*quietly*)   With all oul lumps you do make it, never minding flavour. *And* no spoon.

Pato *gives* **Mag** *her porridge and sits at the table.*

Pato   There you go, now. (*Pause.*) Whatever happened to your hand there, Mrs? Red raw, it is.

Mag   Me hand, is it?

Pato   Was it a scould you did get?

Mag   It *was* a scould.

Pato   You have to be careful with scoulds at your age.

Mag   Careful, is it? Uh-huh . . .

Maureen *enters from the hall, wearing only a bra and slip, and goes over to* **Pato**.

Maureen   Careful what? We was careful, weren't we, Pato?

Maureen *sits across* **Pato**'s *lap.*

Pato (*embarrassed*)   Maureen, now . . .

Maureen   Careful enough, cos we don't need any babies coming, do we? We do have enough babies in this house to be going on with.

Maureen *kisses him at length.* **Mag** *watches in disgust.*

Pato   Maureen, now . . .

Maureen   Just thanking you for a wonderful night, I am, Pato. Well worth the wait it was. *Well* worth the wait.

Pato (*embarrassed*)   Good-oh.

Mag   Discussing me scoulded hand we was before you breezed in with no clothes!

Maureen Ar, feck your scoulded hand. (*To* **Pato**.) You'll have to be putting that thing of yours in me again before too long is past, Pato. I do have a taste for it now, I do...

Pato Maureen...

She kisses him, gets off, and stares at **Mag** *as she passes into the kitchen.*

Maureen A mighty oul taste. Uh-huh.

Pato *gets up and idles around in embarrassment.*

Pato Em, I'll have to be off now in a minute anyways. I do have packing to do I do, and whatyoucall...

Mag (*pointing at* **Maureen**. *Loudly*) *She*'s the one that scoulded me hand! I'll tell you that, now! Let alone sitting on stray men! Held it down on the range she did! Poured chip-pan fat o'er it! Aye, and told the doctor it was me!

Maureen (*pause. Nonplussed, to* **Pato**) Be having a mug of tea before you go, Pato, now.

Pato (*pause*) Maybe a quick one.

Maureen *pours out the tea.* **Mag** *looks back and forth between the two of them.*

Mag Did you not hear what I said?!

Maureen Do you think Pato listens to the smutterings of a senile oul hen?

Mag Senile, is it? (*She holds up her left hand.*) Don't I have the evidence?

Maureen Come over here a second, Pato. I want you to smell this sink for me.

Mag Sinks have nothing to do with it!

Maureen Come over here now, Pato.

Pato Eh?

Pato *goes into the kitchen.*

Maureen Smell that sink.

Pato *leans into the sink, sniffs it, then pulls his head away in disgust.*

Mag   Nothing to do with it, sinks have!

Maureen   Nothing to do with it, is it? Everything to do with it, *I* think it has. Serves as evidence to the character of me accuser, it does.

Pato   What is that, now? The drains?

Maureen   Not the drains at all. Not the drains at all. Doesn't she pour a potty of wee away down there every morning, though I tell her seven hundred times the lavvy to use, but oh no.

Mag   Me scoulded hand this conversation was, and not wee at all!

Maureen   And doesn't even rinse it either. Now is that hygienic? And she does have a urine infection too, is even less hygienic. I wash me praities in there. Here's your tea now, Pato.

Pato *takes his tea, sipping it squeamishly.*

Mag   Put some clothes on you, going around the house half-naked! Would be more in your line!

Maureen   I do like going around the house half-naked. It does turn me on, it does.

Mag   I suppose it does, aye.

Maureen   It does.

Mag   And reminds you of Difford Hall in England, too, I'll bet it does ...

Maureen (*angrily*)   Now you just shut your fecking ...

Mag   None of your own clothes they let you wear in there either, did they?

Maureen   Shut your oul gob, I said ... !

Mag   Only long oul gowns and buckle-down jackets ...

Maureen *approaches* **Mag**, *fists clenched.* **Pato** *catches her arm and steps between the two.*

Pato   What's the matter with ye two at all, now ... ?

Mag   Difford Hall! Difford Hall! Difford Hall . . . !

Maureen   Difford Hall, uh-huh. And I suppose . . .

Mag   Difford Hall! Difford Hall . . . !

Maureen   And I suppose that potty of wee was just a figment of me imagination?

Mag   Forget wee! Forget wee! D'you want to know what Difford Hall is, fella?

Maureen   Shut up, now!

Mag   It's a nut-house! An oul nut-house in England I did have to sign her out of and promise to keep her in me care. Would you want to be seeing the papers now?

Mag *shuffles off to the hall.*

As proof, like. Or to prove am I just a senile oul hen, like, or *who*'s the loopy one? Heh! Pegging wee in me face, oh aye . . .

Quiet pause. **Maureen** *idles over to the table and sits.* **Pato** *pours his tea down the sink, rinses his mug and washes his hands.*

Maureen (*quietly*)   It's true I was in a home there a while, now, after a bit of a breakdown I had. Years ago this is.

Pato   What harm a breakdown, sure? Lots of people do have breakdowns.

Maureen   A lot of doolally people, aye.

Pato   Not doolally people at all. A lot of well-educated people have breakdowns too. In fact, if you're well-educated it's even more likely. Poor Spike Milligan, isn't he forever having breakdowns? He hardly stops. I do have trouble with me nerves every now and then, too, I don't mind admitting. There's no shame at all in that. Only means you do think about things, and take them to heart.

Maureen   No shame in being put in a nut-house a month? Ah no.

Pato   No shame in thinking about things and worrying about things, I'm saying, and 'nut-house' is a silly word to be using, and you know that well enough, now, Maureen.

Maureen   I do.

Pato *goes over and sits across the table from her.*

Maureen   In England I was, this happened. Cleaning work.
When I was twenty-five. Me first time over. Me only time
over. Me sister had just got married, me other sister just about
to. Over in Leeds I was, cleaning offices. Bogs. A whole group
of us, only them were all English. 'Ya oul backward Paddy
fecking . . . The fecking pig's-backside face on ya.' The first
time out of Connemara this was I'd been. 'Get back to that
backward fecking pigsty of yours or whatever hole it was you
drug yourself out of.' Half of the swearing I didn't even
understand. I had to have a black woman explain it to me.
Trinidad she was from. They'd have a go at her too, but she'd
just laugh. This big face she had, this big oul smile. And photos
of Trinidad she'd show me, and 'What the hell have you left
there for?' I'd say. 'To come to this place, cleaning shite?' And
a calendar with a picture of Connemara on I showed her one
day, and 'What the hell have you left there for?' she said back
to me. 'To come to this place . . . ' (*Pause.*) But she moved to
London then, her husband was dying. And after that it all just
got to me.

Pato (*pause*)   That's all past and behind you now anyways,
Maureen.

Pause. **Maureen** *looks at him a while.*

Maureen   Am I still a nut case you're saying, or you're
wondering?

Pato   Not at all, now . . .

Maureen   Oh no . . . ?

Maureen *gets up and wanders back to the kitchen.*

Pato   Not at all. That's a long time in the past is all I'm
saying. And nothing to be ashamed of. Put it behind you, you
should.

Maureen   Put it behind me, aye, with that one hovering
eyeing me every minute, like I'm some kind of . . . some kind of
. . . (*Pause.*) And, no, I didn't scould her oul hand, no matter

how doolally I ever was. Trying to cook chips on her own, she was. We'd argued, and I'd left her on her own an hour, and chips she up and decided she wanted. She must've tipped the pan over. God knows how, the eej. I just found her lying there. Only, because of Difford Hall, she thinks any accusation she throws at me I won't be any the wiser. I won't be able to tell the differ, what's true and what's not. Well, I *am* able to tell the differ. Well able, the smelly oul bitch.

Pato   You shouldn't let her get to you, Maureen.

Maureen   How can I help it, Pato? She's enough to drive anyone loopy, if they weren't loopy to begin with.

Pato (*smiling*)   She is at that, I suppose.

Maureen (*smiling*)   She is. It's surprised I am how sane I've turned out!

They both smile. Pause.

Pato   I *will* have to be off in a minute now, Maureen.

Maureen   Okay, Pato. Did you finish your tea, now?

Pato   I didn't. The talk of your mother's wee, it did put me off it.

Maureen   It would. It would anybody. Don't I have to live with it? (*Sadly.*) Don't I have to live with it? (*Looking straight at him.*) I suppose I do, now.

Pato (*pause*)   Be putting on some clothes there, Maureen. You'll freeze with no fire down.

Pause. **Maureen**'s *mood has become sombre again. She looks down at herself.*

Maureen (*quietly*)   'Be putting on some clothes'? Is it ugly you think I am now, so, 'Be putting on some clothes . . .'

Pato   No, Maureen, the cold, I'm saying. You can't go walking about . . . You'll freeze, sure.

Maureen   It wasn't ugly you thought I was last night, or maybe it was, now.

Pato   No, Maureen, now. What . . . ?

Maureen A beauty queen you thought I was last night, or you said I was. When it's 'Cover yourself', now, 'You do sicken me' . . .

Pato (*approaching her*)   Maureen, no, now, what are you saying that for . . . ?

Maureen Maybe that was the reason so.

Pato (*stops*)   The reason what?

Maureen Be off with you so, if I sicken you.

Pato You don't sicken me.

Maureen (*almost crying*)   Be off with you, I said.

Pato (*approaching again*)   Maureen . . .

Mag *enters, waving papers, stopping* **Pato**'s *approach.*

Mag Eh? Here's the papers now, Difford Hall, if I'm such a senile oul hen. Eh? Who wants an oul read, now? Eh? Proof this is, let alone pegging sinks at me! (*Pause.*) Eh?

Pato Maureen . . .

Maureen (*composed. Gently*)   Be going now, Pato.

Pato (*pause*)   I'll write to you from England. (*Pause. Sternly.*) Look at me! (*Pause. Softly.*) I'll write to you from England.

Pato *puts on his jacket, turns for a last look at* **Maureen**, *then exits, closing the door behind him. Footsteps away. Pause.*

Mag He won't write at all. (*Pause.*) And I did throw your oul dress in that dirty corner too!

Pause. **Maureen** *looks at her a moment, sad, despairing but not angry.*

Maureen Why? Why? Why do you . . . ?

Pause. **Maureen** *goes over to where her dress is lying, crouches down beside it and picks it up, holding it to her chest. She lingers there a moment, then gets up and passes her mother.*

Just look at yourself.

Maureen *exits into hall.*

Mag   Just look at *your*self too, would be . . . would be . . .
(**Maureen** *shuts the hall door behind her.*) . . . more in your line.

Mag *is still holding up the papers rather dumbly. Pause. She lays the
papers down, scratches herself, notices her uneaten porridge and sticks a
finger in it. Quietly.*

Me porridge is gone cold now. (*Loudly.*) Me porridge is gone
cold now!

Mag *stares out front, blankly. Blackout.*

Interval.

Scene Five

Most of the stage is in darkness apart from a spotlight or some such on
Pato *sitting at the table as if in a bedsit in England, reciting a letter he
has written to* **Maureen**.

Pato   Dear Maureen, it is Pato Dooley and I'm writing from
London, and I'm sorry it's taken so long to write to you but to
be honest I didn't know whether you wanted me to one way or
the other, so I have taken it upon myself to try and see. There
are a lot of things I want to say but I am no letter-writer but I
will try to say them if I can. Well, Maureen, there is no major
news here, except a Wexford man on the site a day ago, a rake
of bricks fell on him from the scaffold and forty stitches he did
have in his head and was lucky to be alive at all, he was an old
fella, or fifty-odd anyways, but apart from that there is no
major news. I do go out for a pint of a Saturday or a Friday but
I don't know nobody and don't speak to anyone. There is no
one to speak to. The gangerman does pop his head in
sometimes. I don't know if I've spelt it right, 'Gangerman', is
it 'e-r' or is it 'a'? It is not a word we was taught in school. Well,
Maureen, I am 'beating around the bush' as they say, because
it is you and me I do want to be talking about, if there is such a
thing now as 'you and me', I don't know the state of play.
What I thought I thought we were getting on royally, at the
goodbye to the Yanks and the part after when we did talk and

went to yours. And I *did* think you were a beauty queen and I *do* think, and it wasn't anything to do with that at all or with you at all, I think you thought it was. All it was, it has happened to me a couple of times before when a drink I've taken and was nothing to do with did I want to. I would have been honoured to be the first one you chose, and flattered, and the thing that I'm saying, I was honoured then and I am still honoured, and just because it was not to be that night, does it mean it is not to be ever? I don't see why it should, and I don't see why you was so angry when you was so nice to me when it happened. I think you thought I looked at you differently when your breakdown business came up, when I didn't look at you differently at all, or the thing I said 'Put on your clothes, it's cold', when you seemed to think I did not want to be looking at you in your bra and slip there, when nothing could be further from the truth, because if truth be told I could have looked at you in your bra and slip until the cows came home. I could never get my fill of looking at you in your bra and slip, and some day, God-willing, I will be looking at you in your bra and slip again. Which leads me on to my other thing, unless you still haven't forgiven me, in which case we should just forget about it and part as friends, but if you *have* forgiven me it leads me on to my other thing which I was lying to you before when I said I had no news because I do have news. What the news is I have been in touch with me uncle in Boston and the incident with the Wexford man with the bricks was just the final straw. You'd be lucky to get away with your life the building sites in England, let alone the bad money and the 'You oul Irish this-and-that', and I have been in touch with me uncle in Boston and a job he has offered me there, and I am going to take him up on it. Back in Leenane two weeks tomorrow I'll be, to collect up my stuff and I suppose a bit of a do they'll throw me, and the thing I want to say to you is do you want to come with me? Not straight away of course, I know, because you would have things to clear up, but after a month or two I'm saying, but maybe you haven't forgiven me at all and it's being a fool I'm being. Well, if you haven't forgiven me I suppose it'd be best if we just kept out of each other's way the few days I'm over and if I don't hear from you

I will understand, but if you *have* forgiven me what's to keep you in Ireland? There's your sisters could take care of your mother and why should you have had the burden all these years, don't you deserve a life? And if they say no, isn't there the home in Oughterard isn't ideal but they do take good care of them, my mother before she passed, and don't they have bingo and what good to your mother does that big hill do? No good. (*Pause.*) Anyways, Maureen, I will leave it up to you. My address is up the top there and the number of the phone in the hall, only let it ring a good while if you want to ring and you'll need the codes, and it would be grand to hear from you. If I don't hear from you, I will understand. Take good care of yourself, Maureen. And that night we shared, even if nothing happened, it still makes me happy just to think about it, being close to you, and even if I never hear from you again I'll always have a happy memory of that night, and that's all I wanted to say to you. Do think about it. Yours sincerely, Pato Dooley.

Spotlight cuts out, but while the stage is in darkness **Pato** *continues with a letter to his brother.*

Dear Raymond, how are you? I'm enclosing a bunch of letters I don't want different people snooping in on. Will you hand them out for me and don't be reading them, I know you won't be. The one to Mick Dowd you can wait till he comes out of hospital. That must be an awful thing, almost drowning in silage. The one to poor Girleen you can give to her any time you see her, it is only to tell her to stop falling in love with priests. But the one to Maureen Folan I want you to go over there the day you get this and put it in her hand. This is important now, in her hand put it. Not much other news here. I'll fill you in on more of the America details nearer the time. Yes, it's a great thing. Good luck to you, Raymond, and P.S. Remember now, in Maureen's hand put it. Goodbye.

Scene Six

Afternoon. **Ray** *is standing near the lit range, watching TV, somewhat engrossed, tapping a sealed envelope against his knee now and then.* **Mag** *watches him and the letter from the rocking-chair. Long pause before* **Ray** *speaks.*

Ray   That Wayne's an oul bastard.

Mag   Is he?

Ray   He is. He never stops.

Mag   Oh-h.

Ray (*pause*)   D'you see Patricia with the hair? Patricia's bad enough, but Wayne's a pure terror. (*Pause.*) I do like *Sons and Daughters*, I do.

Mag   Do ya?

Ray   Everybody's always killing each other and a lot of the girls do have swimsuits. That's the best kind of programme.

Mag   I'm just waiting for the news to come on.

Ray (*pause*)   You'll have a long wait.

The programme ends. **Ray** *stretches himself.*

That's that then.

Mag   Is the news not next? Ah no.

Ray   No. For God's sake, *A Country Fecking Practice*'s on next. Isn't it Thursday?

Mag   Turn it off, so, if the news isn't on. That's all I do be waiting for.

Ray *turns the TV off and idles around.*

Ray   Six o'clock the news isn't on 'til. (*He glances at his watch. Quietly, irritated.*) Feck, feck, feck, feck, feck, feck, feck, feck, feck. (*Pause.*) You said she'd be home be now, didn't you?

Mag   I did. (*Pause.*) Maybe she got talking to somebody, although she doesn't usually get talking to somebody. She does keep herself to herself.

Ray I know well she does keep herself to herself. (*Pause.*)
Loopy that woman is, if you ask me. Didn't she keep the tennis
ball that came off me and Mairtin Hanlon's swingball set and
landed in yere fields and wouldn't give it back no matter how
much we begged and that was ten years ago and I still haven't
forgotten it?

Mag I do have no comment, as they say.

Ray Still haven't forgotten it and I never will forget it!

Mag But wasn't it that you and Mairtin were pegging yere
tennis ball at our chickens and clobbered one of them dead is
why your ball was in our fields . . . ?

Ray It was swingball we were playing, Mrs!

Mag Oh-h.

Ray Not clobbering at all. Swingball it was. And never
again able to play swingball were we. For the rest of our youth,
now. For what use is a swingball set without a ball?

Mag No use.

Ray No use is right! No use at all. (*Pause.*) *Bitch!*

Mag (*pause*) Be off and give your letter to me so, Ray, now,
and I'll make sure she gets it, and not have you waiting for a
lass ruined your swingball set on you.

Ray *thinks about it, tempted, but grudgingly decides against it.*

Ray I'm under strict instructions now, Mrs.

Mag (*tuts*) Make me a mug of tea so.

Ray I'm not making you a mug of tea. Under duress is all
I'm here. I'm not skivvying about on top of it.

Mag (*pause*) Or another bit of turf on the fire put. I'm cold.

Ray Did I not just say?

Mag Ah g'wan, Ray. You're a good boy, God bless you.

Sighing, **Ray** *puts the letter – which* **Mag** *stares at throughout – on the
table and uses the heavy black poker beside the range to pick some turf up
and place it inside, stoking it afterwards.*

Ray Neverminding swingball, I saw her there on the road the other week and I said hello to her and what did she do? She outright ignored me. Didn't even look up.

Mag Didn't she?

Ray And what I thought of saying, I thought of saying, 'Up your oul hole, Mrs', but I didn't say it, I just thought of saying it, but thinking back on it I should've gone ahead and said it and skitter on the bitch!

Mag It would've been good enough for her to say it, up and ignoring you on the road, because you're a good gosawer, Ray, fixing me fire for me. Ah, she's been in a foul oul mood lately.

Ray She does wear horrible clothes. And everyone agrees. (*Finished at the range, poker still in hand,* **Ray** *looks over the tea-towel on the back wall.*) 'May you be half an hour in Heaven afore the Devil knows you're dead.'

Mag Aye.

Ray (*funny voice*) 'May you be half an hour in Heaven afore the Devil knows you're dead.'

Mag (*embarrassed laugh*) Aye.

Ray *idles around a little, wielding the poker.*

Ray This is a great oul poker, this is.

Mag Is it?

Ray Good and heavy.

Mag Heavy and long.

Ray Good and heavy and long. A half a dozen coppers you could take out with this poker and barely notice and have not a scratch on it and then clobber them again just for the fun of seeing the blood running out of them. (*Pause.*) Will you sell it to me?

Mag I will not. To go battering the polis?

Ray A fiver.

Mag   We do need it for the fire, sure.

Ray *tuts and puts the poker back beside the range.*

Ray   Sure, that poker's just going to waste in this house.

Ray *idles into the kitchen. Her eye on the letter,* **Mag** *slowly gets out of her chair.*

Ah, I could get a dozen pokers in town just as good if I wanted, and at half the price.

Just as **Mag** *starts her approach to the letter,* **Ray** *returns, not noticing her, idles past and picks the letter back up on his way.* **Mag** *grimaces slightly and sits back down.* **Ray** *opens the front door, glances out to see if* **Maureen** *is coming, then closes it again, sighing.*

A whole afternoon I'm wasting here. (*Pause.*) When I could be at home watching telly.

Ray *sits at the table.*

Mag   You never know, it might be evening before she's ever home.

Ray (*angrily*)   You said three o'clock it was sure to be when I first came in!

Mag   Aye, three o'clock it usually is, oh aye. (*Pause.*) Just sometimes it does be evening. On occasion, like. (*Pause.*) Sometimes it does be *late* evening. (*Pause.*) Sometimes it does be *night*. (*Pause.*) *Morning* it was one time before she . . .

Ray (*interrupting angrily*)   All right, all right! It's thumping you in a minute I'll be!

Mag (*pause*)   I'm only saying now.

Ray   Well, stop saying! (*Sighs. Long pause.*) This house does smell of pee, this house does.

Mag (*pause. Embarrassed*)   Em, cats do get in.

Ray   Do cats get in?

Mag   They do. (*Pause.*) They do go to the sink.

Ray (*pause*)   What do they go to the sink for?

Mag   To wee.

Ray   To wee? They go to the sink to wee? (*Piss-taking.*) Sure, that's mighty good of them. You do get a very considerate breed of cat up this way so.

Mag (*pause*)   I don't know what breed they are.

Pause. **Ray** *lets his head slump down onto the table with a bump, and slowly and rhythmically starts banging his fist down beside it.*

Ray (*droning*)   I don't want to be here, I don't want to be here, I don't want to be here, I don't want to be here . . .

Ray *lifts his head back up, stares at the letter, then starts slowly turning it around, end over end, sorely tempted.*

Mag (*pause*)   Do me a mug of tea, Ray. (*Pause.*) Or a mug of Complan do me, even. (*Pause.*) And give it a good stir to get rid of the oul lumps.

Ray   If it was getting rid of oul lumps I was to be, it wouldn't be with Complan I'd be starting. It would be much closer to home, boy. Oh aye, much closer. A big lump sitting in an oul fecking rocking-chair it would be. I'll tell you that!

Mag (*pause*)   Or a Cup-a-Soup do me.

Ray *grits his teeth and begins breathing in and out through them, almost crying.*

Ray (*giving in sadly*)   Pato, Pato, Pato. (*Pause.*) Ah what news could it be? (*Pause. Sternly.*) Were I to leave this letter here with you, Mrs, it would be straight to that one you would be giving it, isn't that right?

Mag   It is. Oh, straight to Maureen I'd be giving it.

Ray (*pause*)   And it isn't opening it you would be?

Mag   It is not. Sure, a letter is a private thing. If it isn't my name on it, what business would it be of mine?

Ray   And may God strike you dead if you do open it?

Mag   And may God strike me dead if I do open it, only He'll have no need to strike me dead because I won't be opening it.

Ray (*pause*) I'll leave it so.

Ray *stands, places the letter up against a salt-cellar, thinks about it again for a moment, looks* **Mag** *over a second, looks back at the letter again, thinks once more, then waves a hand in a gesture of tired resignation, deciding to leave it.*

I'll be seeing you then, Mrs.

Mag Be seeing you, Pato. *Ray*, I mean.

Ray *grimaces at her again and exits through the front door, but leaves it slightly ajar, as he is still waiting outside.* **Mag** *places her hands on the sides of the rocking-chair, about to drag herself up, then warily remembers she hasn't heard* **Ray**'s *footsteps away. She lets her hands rest back in her lap and sits back serenely. Pause. The front door bursts open and* **Ray** *sticks his head around it to look at her. She smiles at him innocently.*

Ray Good-oh.

Ray *exits again, closing the door behind him fully this time.* **Mag** *listens to his footsteps fading away, then gets up, picks up the envelope and opens it, goes back to the range and lifts off the lid so that the flames are visible, and stands there reading the letter. She drops the first short page into the flames as she finishes it, then starts reading the second. Slow fade-out.*

Scene Seven

Night. **Mag** *is in her rocking-chair,* **Maureen** *at the table, reading. The radio is on low, tuned to a request show. The reception is quite poor, wavering and crackling with static. Pause before* **Mag** *speaks.*

Mag A poor reception.

Maureen Can I help it if it's a poor reception?

Mag (*pause*) Crackly. (*Pause.*) We can hardly hear the tunes. (*Pause.*) We can hardly hear what are the dedications or from what part of the country.

Maureen I can hear well enough.

Mag   Can ya?

Maureen (*pause*)   Maybe it's deaf it is you're going.

Mag   It's not deaf I'm going. Not nearly deaf.

Maureen   It's a home for deaf people I'll have to be putting you in soon. (*Pause.*) And it isn't cod in butter sauce you'll be getting in there. No. Not by a long chalk. Oul beans on toast or something is all you'll be getting in there. If you're lucky. And then if you don't eat it, they'll give you a good kick, or maybe a punch.

Mag (*pause*)   I'd die before I'd let meself be put in a home.

Maureen   Hopefully, aye.

Mag (*pause*)   That was a nice bit of cod in butter sauce, Maureen.

Maureen   I suppose it was.

Mag   Tasty.

Maureen   All I do is boil it in the bag and snip it with a scissor. I hardly need your compliments.

Mag (*pause*)   Mean to me is all you ever are nowadays.

Maureen   If I am or if I'm not. (*Pause.*) Didn't I buy you a packet of wine gums last week if I'm so mean?

Mag (*pause*)   All because of Pato Dooley you're mean, I suppose. (*Pause.*) Him not inviting you to his oul going-away do tonight.

Maureen   Pato Dooley has his own life to lead.

Mag   Only after one thing that man was.

Maureen   Maybe he was, now. Or maybe it was me who was only after one thing. We do have equality nowadays. Not like in your day.

Mag   There was nothing wrong in my day.

Maureen   Allowed to go on top of a man nowadays, we are. All we have to do is ask. And nice it is on top of a man, too.

Mag Is it nice now, Maureen?

Maureen (*bemused that* **Mag** *isn't offended*) It is.

Mag It does sound nice. Ah, good enough for yourself, now.

Maureen, *still bemused, gets some shortbread fingers from the kitchen and eats a couple.*

Mag And not worried about having been put in the family way, are you?

Maureen I'm not. We was careful.

Mag Was ye careful?

Maureen Aye. We was nice and careful. We was *lovely* and careful, if you must know.

Mag I'll bet ye was lovely and careful, aye. Oh aye. Lovely and careful, I'll bet ye were.

Maureen (*pause*) You haven't been sniffing the paraffin lamps again?

Mag (*pause*) It's always the paraffin lamp business you do throw at me.

Maureen It's a funny oul mood you're in so.

Mag Is it a funny oul mood? No. Just a normal mood, now.

Maureen It's a funny one. (*Pause.*) Aye, a great oul time me and Pato did have. I can see now what all the fuss did be about, but ah, there has to be more to a man than just being good in bed. Things in common too you do have to have, y'know, like what books do you be reading, or what are your politics and the like, so I did have to tell him it was no-go, no matter how good in bed he was.

Mag When was this you did tell him?

Maureen A while ago it was I did tell him. Back . . .

Mag (*interrupting*) And I suppose he was upset at that.

Maureen He *was* upset at that but I assured him it was for the best and he did seem to accept it then.

Mag   I'll bet he accepted it.

Maureen (*pause*)   But that's why I thought it would be unfair of me to go over to his do and wish him goodbye. I thought it would be awkward for him.

Mag   It would be awkward for him, aye, I suppose. Oh aye. (*Pause.*) So all it was was ye didn't have enough things in common was all that parted ye?

Maureen   Is all it was. And parted on amicable terms, and with no grudges on either side. (*Pause.*) No. No grudges at all. I did get what I did want out of Pato Dooley that night, and that was good enough for him, and that was good enough for me.

Mag   Oh aye, now. I'm sure. It was good enough for the both of ye. Oh aye.

Mag *smiles and nods.*

Maureen (*laughing*)   It's a crazy oul mood you're in for yourself tonight!

Pause.

Pleased that tonight it is Pato's leaving and won't be coming pawing me again is what it is, I bet.

Mag   Maybe that's what it is. I *am* glad Pato's leaving.

Maureen (*smiling*)   An interfering oul biddy is all you are. (*Pause.*) Do you want a shortbread finger?

Mag   I *do* want a shortbread finger.

Maureen   Please.

Mag   Please.

Maureen *gives* **Mag** *a shortbread finger, after waving it phallically in the air a moment.*

Maureen   Remind me of something, shortbread fingers do.

Mag   I suppose they do, now.

Maureen I suppose it's so long since you've seen what they remind me of, you do forget what they look like.

Mag I suppose I do. And I suppose you're the expert.

Maureen I am the expert.

Mag Oh aye.

Maureen I'm the king of the experts.

Mag I suppose you are, now. Oh, I'm sure. I suppose you're the king of the experts.

Maureen (*pause. Suspicious*) Why wouldn't you be sure?

Mag With your Pato Dooley and your throwing it all in me face like an oul peahen, eh? When . . . (**Mag** *catches herself before revealing any more.*)

Maureen (*pause. Smiling*) When what?

Mag Not another word on the subject am I saying. I do have no comment, as they say. This is a nice shortbread finger.

Maureen (*with an edge*) When what, now?

Mag (*getting scared*) When nothing, Maureen.

Maureen (*forcefully*) No, when what, now? (*Pause.*) Have you been speaking to somebody?

Mag Who would I be speaking to, Maureen?

Maureen (*trying to work it out*) You've been speaking to somebody. You've . . .

Mag Nobody have I been speaking to, Maureen. You know well I don't be speaking to anybody. And, sure, who would Pato be telling about that . . . ?

Mag *suddenly realises what she's said.* **Maureen** *stares at her in dumb shock and hate, then walks to the kitchen, dazed, puts a chip-pan on the stove, turns it on high and pours a half-bottle of cooking oil into it, takes down the rubber gloves that are hanging on the back wall and puts them on.* **Mag** *puts her hands on the arms of the rocking-chair to drag herself up, but* **Maureen** *shoves a foot against her stomach and groin, ushering her back.* **Mag** *leans back into the chair, frightened, staring at*

Maureen, *who sits at the table, waiting for the oil to boil. She speaks quietly, staring straight ahead.*

Maureen How do you know?

Mag Nothing do I know, Maureen.

Maureen Uh-huh?

Mag (*pause*) Or was it Ray did mention something? Aye, I think it was Ray . . .

Maureen Nothing to Ray would Pato've said about that subject.

Mag (*tearfully*) Just to stop you bragging like an oul peahen, was I saying, Maureen. Sure what does an oul woman like me know? Just guessing, I was.

Maureen You know sure enough, and guessing me arse, and not on me face was it written. For the second time and for the last time I'll be asking, now. How do you know?

Mag On your face it *was* written, Maureen. Sure that's the only way I knew. You still do have the look of a virgin about you you always have had. (*Without malice.*) You always will.

Pause. The oil has started boiling. **Maureen** *rises, turns the radio up, stares at* **Mag** *as she passes her, takes the pan off the boil and turns the gas off, and returns to* **Mag** *with it.*

(*Terrified.*) A letter he did send you I read!

Maureen *slowly and deliberately takes her mother's shrivelled hand, holds it down on the burning range, and starts slowly pouring some of the hot oil over it, as* **Mag** *screams in pain and terror.*

Maureen Where is the letter?

Mag (*through screams*) I did burn it! I'm sorry, Maureen!

Maureen What did the letter say?

Mag *is screaming so much that she can't answer.* **Maureen** *stops pouring the oil and releases the hand, which* **Mag** *clutches to herself, doubled-up, still screaming, crying and whimpering.*

Maureen What did the letter say?

Mag   Said he did have too much to drink, it did! Is why, and not your fault at all.

Maureen   And what else did it say?

Mag   He won't be putting me into no home!

Maureen   What are you talking about, no home? What else did it say?!

Mag   I can't remember, now, Maureen. I *can't* ...!

Maureen *grabs* **Mag**'s *hand, holds it down again and repeats the torture.*

Mag   No ...!

Maureen   What else did it say?! Eh?!

Mag (*through screams*)   Asked you to go to America with him, it did!

Stunned, **Maureen** *releases* **Mag**'s *hand and stops pouring the oil.* **Mag** *clutches her hand to herself again, whimpering.*

Maureen   What?

Mag   But how could you go with him? You do still have me to look after.

Maureen (*in a happy daze*)   He asked me to go to America with him? Pato asked me to go to America with him?

Mag (*looking up at her*)   But what about me, Maureen?

A slight pause before **Maureen**, *in a single and almost lazy motion, throws the considerable remainder of the oil into* **Mag**'s *midriff, some of it splashing up into her face.* **Mag** *doubles-up, screaming, falls to the floor, trying to pat the oil off her, and lies there convulsing, screaming and whimpering.* **Maureen** *steps out of her way to avoid her fall, still in a daze, barely noticing her.*

Maureen (*dreamily, to herself*)   He asked me to go to America with him ...? (*Recovering herself.*) What time is it? Oh feck, he'll be leaving! I've got to see him. Oh God ... What will I wear? Uh ... Me black dress! Me little black dress! It'll be a remembrance to him ...

Maureen *darts off through the hall.*

Mag (*quietly, sobbing*)   Maureen ... help me ...

Maureen *returns a moment later, pulling her black dress on.*

Maureen (*to herself*)   How do I look? Ah, I'll have to do. What time is it? Oh God ...

Mag   Help me, Maureen ...

Maureen (*brushing her hair*)   Help you, is it? After what you've done? Help you, she says. No, I won't help you, and I'll tell you another thing. If you've made me miss Pato before he goes, then you'll *really* be for it, so you will, and no messing this time. Out of me fecking way, now ...

Maureen *steps over* **Mag**, *who is still shaking on the floor, and exits through the front door. Pause.* **Mag** *is still crawling around slightly. The front door bangs open and* **Mag** *looks up at* **Maureen** *as she breezes back in.*

Me car keys I forgot ...

Maureen *grabs her keys from the table, goes to the door, turns back to the table and switches the radio off.*

Electricity.

Maureen *exits again, slamming the door. Pause. Sound of her car starting and pulling off. Pause.*

Mag (*quietly*)   But who'll look after me, so?

Mag, *still shaking, looks down at her scalded hand. Blackout.*

Scene Eight

Same night. The only light in the room emanates from the orange coals through the grill of the range, just illuminating the dark shapes of **Mag**, *sitting in her rocking-chair, which rocks back and forth of its own volition, her body unmoving, and* **Maureen**, *still in her black dress, who idles very slowly around the room, poker in hand.*

Maureen   To Boston. To Boston I'll be going. Isn't that where them two were from, the Kennedys, or was that somewhere else, now? Robert Kennedy I did prefer over Jack Kennedy. He seemed to be nicer to women. Although I haven't read up on it. (*Pause.*) Boston. It does have a nice ring to it. Better than England it'll be, I'm sure. Although where wouldn't be better than England? No shite I'll be cleaning there, anyways, and no names called, and Pato'll be there to have a say-so anyways if there was to be names called, but I'm sure there won't be. The Yanks do love the Irish. (*Pause.*) Almost begged me, Pato did. Almost on his hands and knees, he was, near enough crying. At the station I caught him, not five minutes to spare, thanks to you. Thanks to your oul interfering. But too late to be interfering you are now. Oh aye. Be far too late, although you did give it a good go, I'll say that for you. Another five minutes and you'd have had it. Poor you. Poor selfish oul bitch, oul you. (*Pause.*) Kissed the face off me, he did, when he saw me there. Them blue eyes of his. Them muscles. Them arms wrapping me. 'Why did you not answer me letter?' And all for coming over and giving you a good kick he was when I told him, but 'Ah no,' I said, 'isn't she just a feeble-minded oul feck, not worth dirtying your boots on?' I was defending you there. (*Pause.*) 'You will come to Boston with me so, me love, when you get up the money.' 'I will, Pato. Be it married or be it living in sin, what do I care? What do I care if tongues'd be wagging? Tongues have wagged about me before, let them wag again. Let them never stop wagging, so long as I'm with you, Pato, what do I care about tongues? So long as it's you and me, and the warmth of us cuddled up, and the skins of us asleep, is all I ever really wanted anyway.' (*Pause.*) 'Except we do still have a problem, what to do with your oul mam, there,' he said. 'Would an oul folks home be too harsh?' 'It wouldn't be too harsh but it would be too expensive.' 'What about your sisters so?' 'Me sisters wouldn't have the bitch. Not even a half-day at Christmas to be with her can them two stand. They clear forgot her birthday this year as well as that. 'How do you stick her without going off your rocker?' they do say to me. Behind her back, like. (*Pause.*) 'I'll leave it up to yourself so,' Pato says. He was on the train be this time, we was kissing out the window, like they do in films. 'I'll leave it up to yourself so, whatever you decide. If it takes a month, let it take a month. And if it's finally you decide you can't bear to be parted from her and have to stay behind, well, I can't say I would like it, but I'd understand. But if even a year it has to take for you to decide, it is a year I will be waiting, and won't be minding the wait.' 'It won't be a year it is you'll be waiting, Pato', I called out then, the train was pulling away. 'It won't be a year nor yet nearly a year. It won't be a week!'

The rocking-chair has stopped its motions. **Mag** *starts to slowly lean forward at the waist until she finally topples over and falls heavily to the floor, dead. A red chunk of skull hangs from a string of skin at the side of her head.* **Maureen** *looks down at her, somewhat bored, taps her on the side with the toe of her shoe, then steps onto her back and stands there in throughtful contemplation.*

'Twas over the stile she did trip. Aye. And down the hill she did fall. Aye. (*Pause.*) Aye.

Pause. Blackout.

Scene Nine

A rainy afternoon. Front door opens and **Maureen** *enters in funeral attire, takes her jacket off and idles around quietly, her mind elsewhere. She lights a fire in the range, turns the radio on low and sits down in the rocking-chair. After a moment she half-laughs, takes down the boxes of Complan and porridge from the kitchen shelf, goes back to the range and empties the contents of both on the fire. She exits into the hall and returns a moment later with an old suitcase which she lays on the table, brushing off a thick layer of dust. She opens it, considers for a second what she needs to pack, then returns to the hall. There is a knock at the door.* **Maureen** *returns, thinks a moment, takes the suitcase off the table and places it to one side, fixes her hair a little, then answers the door.*

Maureen   Oh hello there, Ray.

Ray (*off*)   Hello there, Mrs . . .

Maureen   Come in ahead for yourself.

Ray   I did see you coming ahead up the road.

Ray *enters, closing the door.* **Maureen** *idles to the kitchen and makes herself some tea.*

I didn't think so early you would be back. Did you not want to go on to the reception or the whatyoucall they're having at Rory's so?

Maureen   No. I do have better things to do with me time.

Ray   Aye, aye. Have your sisters gone on to it?

Maureen   They have, aye.

Ray   Of course. Coming back here after, will they be?

Maureen   Going straight home, I think they said they'd be.

Ray   Oh aye. Sure, it's a long oul drive for them. Or fairly long. (*Pause.*) It did all go off okay, then?

Maureen   It did.

Ray   Despite the rain.

Maureen   Despite the rain.

Ray   A poor oul day for a funeral.

Maureen   It was. When it could've been last month we buried her, and she could've got the last of the sun, if it wasn't for the hundred bastarding inquests, proved nothing.

Ray   You'll be glad that's all over and done with now, anyways.

Maureen   Very glad.

Ray   I suppose they do only have their jobs to do. (*Pause.*) Although no fan am I of the bastarding polis. Me two wee toes they went and broke on me for no reason, me arsehole drunk and disorderly.

Maureen   The polis broke your toes, did they?

Ray   They did.

Maureen   Oh. Tom Hanlon said what it was you kicked a door in just your socks.

Ray   Did he now? And I suppose you believe a policeman's word over mine. Oh aye. Isn't that how the Birmingham Six went down?

Maureen   Sure, you can't equate your toes with the Birmingham Six, now, Ray.

Ray   It's the selfsame differ. (*Pause.*) What was I saying, now?

Maureen   Some bull.

Ray   Some bull, is it? No. Asking about your mam's funeral, I was.

Maureen   That's what I'm saying.

Ray (*pause*)   Was there a big turn-out at it?

Maureen   Me sisters and one of their husbands and nobody else but Maryjohnny Rafferty and oul Father Walsh – Welsh – saying the thing.

Ray   Father Welsh punched Mairtin Hanlon in the head once, and for no reason. (*Pause.*) Are you not watching telly for yourself, no?

Maureen   I'm not. It's only Australian oul shite they do ever show on that thing.

Ray (*slightly bemused*)   Sure, that's why I do like it. Who wants to see Ireland on telly?

Maureen   *I* do.

Ray   All you have to do is look out your window to see Ireland. And it's soon bored you'd be. 'There goes a calf.' (*Pause.*) I be bored anyway. I be continually bored. (*Pause.*) London I'm thinking of going to. Aye. Thinking of it, anyways. To work, y'know. One of these days. Or else Manchester. They have a lot more drugs in Manchester. Supposedly, anyways.

Maureen Don't be getting messed up in drugs, now, Ray, for yourself. Drugs are terrible dangerous.

Ray Terrible dangerous, are they? Drugs, now?

Maureen You know full well they are.

Ray Maybe they are, maybe they are. But there are plenty of other things just as dangerous, would kill you just as easy. Maybe even easier.

Maureen (*wary*) Things like what, now?

Ray (*pause. Shrugging*) This bastarding town for one.

Maureen (*pause. Sadly*) Is true enough.

Ray Just that it takes seventy years. Well, it won't take me seventy years. I'll tell you that. No way, boy. (*Pause.*) How old was your mother, now, when she passed?

Maureen Seventy, aye. Bang on.

Ray She had a good innings, anyway. (*Pause.*) Or an innings, anyway. (*Sniffs the air.*) What's this you've been burning?

Maureen Porridge and Complan I've been burning.

Ray For why?

Maureen Because I don't eat porridge or Complan. The remainders of me mother's, they were. I was having a good clear-out.

Ray Only a waste that was.

Maureen Do I need your say-so so?

Ray I'd've been glad to take them off your hands, I'm saying.

Maureen (*quietly*) I don't need your say-so.

Ray The porridge, anyway. I do like a bit of porridge. I'd've left the Complan. I don't drink Complan. Never had no call to.

Maureen   There's some Kimberleys left in the packet I was about to burn too, you can have, if it's such a big thing.

Ray   I *will* have them Kimberleys. I do love Kimberleys.

Maureen   I bet you do.

Ray *eats a couple of Kimberleys.*

Ray   Are they a bit stale, now? (*Chews.*) It does be hard to tell with Kimberleys. (*Pause.*) I think Kimberleys are me favourite biscuits out of any biscuits. Them or Jaffa Cakes. (*Pause.*) Or Wagon Wheels. (*Pause.*) Or would you classify Wagon Wheels as biscuits at all now. Aren't they more of a kind of a bar ... ?

Maureen (*interrupting*)   I've things to do now, Ray. Was it some reason you had to come over or was it just to discuss Wagon Wheels?

Ray   Oh aye, now. No, I did have a letter from Pato the other day and he did ask me to come up.

Maureen *sits in the rocking-chair and listens with keen interest.*

Maureen   He did? What did he have to say?

Ray   He said sorry to hear about your mother and all, and his condolences he sent.

Maureen   Aye, aye, aye, and anything else, now?

Ray   That was the main gist of it, the message he said to pass onto you.

Maureen   It had no times or details, now?

Ray   Times or details? No ...

Maureen   I suppose ...

Ray   Eh?

Maureen   Eh?

Ray   Eh? Oh, also he said he was sorry he didn't get to see you the night he left, there, he would've liked to've said goodbye. But if that was the way you wanted it, so be it. Although rude, too, I thought that was.

Maureen (*standing, confused*)   I did see him the night he left.
At the station, there.

Ray   What station? Be taxicab Pato left. What are you
thinking of?

Maureen (*sitting*)   I don't know now.

Ray   Be taxicab Pato left, and sad that he never got your
goodbye, although why he wanted your goodbye I don't
know. (*Pause.*) I'll tell you this, Maureen, not being harsh, but
your house does smell an awful lot nicer now that your
mother's dead. I'll say it does, now.

Maureen   Well, isn't that the best? With me thinking I did
see him the night he left, there. The train that pulled away.

He looks at her as if she's mad.

Ray   Aye, aye. (*Mumbled, sarcastic.*) Have a rest for yourself.
(*Pause.*) Oh, do you know a lass called, em . . . Dolores Hooley,
or Healey, now? She was over with the Yanks when they was
over.

Maureen   I know the name, aye.

Ray   She was at me uncle's do they had there, dancing with
me brother early on. You remember?

Maureen   Dancing with him, was it? Throwing herself at
him would be nearer the mark. Like a cheap oul whore.

Ray   I don't know about that, now.

Maureen   Like a cheap oul whore. And where did it get her?

Ray   She did seem nice enough to me, there, now. Big brown
eyes she had. And I do like brown eyes, me, I do. Oh aye. Like
the lass used to be on *Bosco*. Or I *think* the lass used to be on
Bosco had brown eyes. We had a black and white telly at that
time. (*Pause.*) What was I talking about, now?

Maureen   Something about this Dolores Hooley or whoever
she fecking is.

Ray   Oh aye. Herself and Pato did get engaged a week ago,
now, he wrote and told me.

Maureen (*shocked*)   Engaged to do what?

Ray   Engaged to get married. What do you usually get engaged for? 'Engaged to do what?' Engaged to eat a bun!

Maureen *is dumbstruck.*

Ray   A bit young for him, I think, but good luck to him. A whirlwind oul whatyoucall. July next year, they're thinking of having it, but I'll have to write and tell him to move it either forward or back, else it'll coincide with the European Championships. I wonder if they'll have the European Championships on telly over there at all? Probably not, now, the Yankee bastards. They don't care about football at all. Ah well. (*Pause.*) It won't be much of a change for her anyways, from Hooley to Dooley. Only one letter. The 'h'. That'll be a good thing. (*Pause.*) Unless it's Healey that she is. I can't remember. (*Pause.*) If it's Healey, it'll be three letters. The 'h', the 'e' and the 'a'. (*Pause.*) Would you want me to be passing any message on, now, when I'm writing, Mrs? I'm writing tomorrow.

Maureen   I get . . . I do get confused. Dolores Hooley . . . ?

Ray (*pause. Irritated*)   Would you want me to be passing on any message, now, I'm saying?

Maureen (*pause*)   Dolores Hooley . . . ?

Ray (*sighing*)   Fecking . . . The loons you do get in this house! Only repeating!

Maureen   Who's a loon?

Ray   Who's a loon, she says!

Ray *scoffs and turns away, looking out the window.* **Maureen** *quietly picks up the poker from beside the range and, holding it low at her side, slowly approaches him from behind.*

Maureen (*angrily*)   Who's a loon?!

Ray *suddenly sees something hidden behind a couple of boxes on the inner window ledge.*

Ray (*angrily*)   Well, isn't that fecking just the fecking best yet . . . !

Ray picks up a faded tennis ball with a string sticking out of it from the ledge and spins around to confront **Maureen** *with it, so angry that he doesn't even notice the poker.* **Maureen** *stops in her tracks.*

Sitting on that fecking shelf all these fecking years you've had it, and what good did it do ya?! A tenner that swingball set did cost me poor ma and da and in 1979 that was, when a tenner was a lot of money. The best fecking present I did ever get and only two oul months' play out of it I got before you went and confiscated it on me. What right did you have? What right at all? No right. And just left it sitting there then to fade to fecking skitter. I wouldn't't've minded if you'd got some use out of it, if you'd taken the string out and played pat-ball or something agin a wall, but no. Just out of pure spite is the only reason you kept it, and right under me fecking nose. And then you go wondering who's a fecking loon? Who's a fecking loon, she says. I'll tell you who's a fecking loon, lady. *You*'re a fecking loon!

Maureen *lets the poker fall to the floor with a clatter and sits in the rocking-chair, dazed.*

Maureen   I don't know why I did keep your swingball on you, Raymond. I can't remember at all, now. I think me head was in a funny oul way in them days.

Ray   'In them days,' she says, as she pegs a good poker on the floor and talks about trains.

Ray *picks the poker up and puts it in its place.*

That's a good poker, that is. Don't be banging it against anything hard like that, now.

Maureen   I won't.

Ray   That's an awful good poker. (*Pause.*) To show there's no hard feelings over me swingball, will you sell me that poker, Mrs? A fiver I'll give you.

Maureen   Ah, I don't want to be selling me poker now, Ray.

Ray   G'wan. Six!

Maureen   No. It does have sentimental value to me.

Ray   I don't forgive you, so!

Maureen   Ah, don't be like that, now, Ray...

Ray   No, I don't forgive you at all...

Ray *goes to the front door and opens it.*

Maureen   Ray! Are you writing to your brother, so?

Ray (*sighing*)   I am. Why?

Maureen   Will you be passing a message on from me?

Ray (*sighs*)   Messages, messages, messages, messages! What's the message, so? And make it a short one.

Maureen   Just say...

Maureen *thinks about it a while.*

Ray   This week, if you can!

Maureen   Just say...Just say, 'The beauty queen of Leenane says hello.' That's all.

Ray   'The beauty queen of Leenane says hello.'

Maureen   Aye. No!

Ray *sighs again.*

Maureen   *Goodbye.* Goodbye. 'The beauty queen of Leenane says *goodbye.*'

Ray   'The beauty queen of Leenane says goodbye.' Whatever the feck that means, I'll pass it on. 'The beauty queen of Leenane says goodbye', although after this fecking swingball business, I don't see why the feck I should. Goodbye to you so, Mrs...

Maureen   Will you turn the radio up a biteen too, before you go, there, Pato, now? *Ray,* I mean...

Ray (*exasperated*)   Feck...

Ray *turns the radio up.*

The exact fecking image of your mother you are, sitting there pegging orders and forgetting me name! Goodbye!

Maureen   And pull the door after you . . .

Ray (*shouting angrily*)   I was going to pull the fecking door after me!!

Ray *slams the door behind him as he exits. Pause.* **Maureen** *starts rocking slightly in the chair, listening to the song by The Chieftains on the radio. The announcer's quiet, soothing voice is then heard.*

Announcer   A lovely tune from The Chieftains there. This next one, now, goes out from Annette and Margo Folan to their mother Maggie, all the way out in the mountains of Leenane, a lovely part of the world there, on the occasion of her seventy-first birthday last month now. Well, we hope you had a happy one, Maggie, and we hope there'll be a good many more of them to come on top of it. I'm sure there will. This one's for you, now.

'*The Spinning Wheel*' *by Delia Murphy is played.* **Maureen** *gently rocks in the chair until about the middle of the fourth verse, when she quietly gets up, picks up the dusty suitcase, caresses it slightly, moves slowly to the hall door and looks back at the empty rocking-chair a while. It is still rocking gently. Slight pause, then* **Maureen** *exits into the hall, closing its door behind her as she goes. We listen to the song on the radio to the end, as the chair gradually stops rocking and the lights, very slowly, fade to black.*

Methuen Modern Plays

include work by

Jean Anouilh
John Arden
Margaretta D'Arcy
Peter Barnes
Sebastian Barry
Brendan Behan
Edward Bond
Bertolt Brecht
Howard Brenton
Simon Burke
Jim Cartwright
Caryl Churchill
Noël Coward
Sarah Daniels
Nick Dear
Shelagh Delaney
David Edgar
Dario Fo
Michael Frayn
John Godber
Paul Godfrey
John Guare
Peter Handke
Jonathan Harvey
Iain Heggie
Declan Hughes
Terry Johnson
Barrie Keeffe
Stephen Lowe
Doug Lucie

John McGrath
David Mamet
Patrick Marber
Arthur Miller
Mtwa, Ngema & Simon
Tom Murphy
Phyllis Nagy
Peter Nichols
Joseph O'Connor
Joe Orton
Louise Page
Joe Penhall
Luigi Pirandello
Stephen Poliakoff
Franca Rame
Philip Ridley
Reginald Rose
David Rudkin
Willy Russell
Jean-Paul Sartre
Sam Shepard
Wole Soyinka
C. P. Taylor
Theatre de Complicite
Theatre Workshop
Sue Townsend
Judy Upton
Timberlake Wertenbaker
Victoria Wood

For a Complete Catalogue of Methuen Drama titles
write to:

Methuen Drama
Michelin House
81 Fulham Road
London SW3 6RB